WEAPON

SNIPER RIFLES

2591.

MARTIN PEGLER

First published in Great Britain in 2010 by Osprey Publishing, Midland House, West Way, Botley, Oxford, OX2 0PH, UK 44-02 23rd Street, Suite 219, Long Island City, NY 11101, USA

E-mail: info@ospreypublishing.com

The front cover images are courtesy of US Army and the author's collection. The images on the title page, p7 and p29 are © Corbis. All images not credited are from the author's collection.

A CIP catalogue record for this book is available from the British Library

Print ISBN: 978 1 84908 398 0

PDF ebook ISBN: 978 1 84908 399 7

Martin Pegler has asserted his right under the Copyright, Designs and Patents Act, 1988, to be identified as the Author of this Work

Page layout by Ben Salvesen

Battlescene artwork by Peter Dennis

Index by Fineline Editorial Services

Typeset in Sabon and Univers

Originated by PDQ Media

Printed in China through World Print Ltd

10 11 12 13 14   10 9 8 7 6 5 4 3 2 1

Dedication
To my wife, Katie, with heartfelt thanks.

Acknowledgements
I am extremely grateful to the following people and organizations: Riflecraft in Norfolk for their technical help, access to rifles and mugs of tea. To Dr Robert Maze, Geoff Sturgess, George Yannaghas, Denny Pizzini and Roy Jinks for supplying photos from their fine collections. Also to the Iron Brigade Armory, the Royal Armouries Leeds, Springfield Armory National Historical Site, the Ministry of Defence, the US Army and US Marine Corps for permission to use photos. Thanks once more to the assorted snipers who helped me with information and prefer, as usual, to remain in the shadows. Lastly, thank you to ex-sniper Harry Furness for yet more priceless information.

www.ospreypublishing.com

Glossary

Armour-piercing: A rifle bullet with a hardened steel core capable of penetrating armour plate.

Ball: The standard-issue, lead-cored jacketed military bullet.

Cartridge: A single unit of ammunition comprising primer, case, propellant and bullet.

Cartridge case: The container, usually brass, that holds the propellant charge.

Crosshair (also graticule or reticule): The intersecting vertical and horizontal lines visible through the telescopic sight that provide the shooter's point of aim.

Elevation drum: The adjuster drum on the top of a scope body that enables the horizontal crosshairs to be raised or lowered.

Knox-form: The flat surface on the rear of a barrel that enables it to be screwed into the receiver using a special spanner or clamp.

Long-action: The internal length of the receiver in which the bolt travels. A long-action rifle can chamber a longer cartridge than a short-action and this provides more possibilities for ammunition upgrades.

Mount: The method of fitting a scope to a rifle, normally by means of rings clamped on the scope body with projecting lugs that fit tightly into steel bases screwed or soldered onto the rifle.

Objective lens: The lens on a telescopic sight furthest away from the shooter's eye.

Ocular lens: The lens on the telescopic sight closest to the shooter's eye.

Offset scope: A telescopic sight mounted on the left side of a rifle to facilitate reloading.

Receiver or action: The main body of the rifle or machine gun containing the bolt or breech-block.

Rimless: A cartridge with an extraction groove cut in its base. Thus the rim is the same diameter as the base.

Rimmed: A cartridge with a projecting rim designed to be gripped by the extractor.

Trajectory: The curving path of a bullet in flight.

Trigger pull: The strength of resistance of the trigger required to release the firing pin and discharge the weapon.

Windage: (A) The propellant gas that bypasses the seated bullet in black-powder firearms (also known as blow-by); (B) The effect of side-wind on a bullet.

Windage drum: The adjuster drum on the side of a scope body that adjusts the vertical crosshair.

Zero (or zeroing): The zero is the point at which the bullet hits the target. It must equate exactly to the position of the crosshair. Zeroing is the act of regularly checking this aim/impact correspondence is correct at a pre-determined distance.

CONTENTS

INTRODUCTION

Blasé as we all can be about technological advances, we tend to forget that the latest shiny gadgets that abound in our modern world would be pointless without the backup that enables them to work. The factors that enable these things to be used are inter-dependent on a complex range of other technologies, most of which are beyond both our comprehension and our control. On an everyday level, how useful is a mobile phone when the batteries run out and what can you do with a car that has no petrol? Far more complicated are the myriad support systems required to make much of our high-end technology function. As a military example, a standard heat-seeking missile requires special fuel, a dedicated warhead, computers that control the guidance system, gyroscopic stabilizing and an on-board self-destruct mechanism. Without all of these, the rocket is simply a scrap-bin of very expensive parts heading into the blue yonder.

Even the sciences that have brought us that most commonplace of military hardware, the firearm, are wholly dependent on external factors that many shooters do not understand. The steel used must be of the correct grade, the barrel must be bored perfectly straight and sights properly aligned. The ammunition has to be consistently manufactured, with reliable primers, high-quality powder and bullets that are identical in weight and shape, and with ballistic properties that exactly match the requirements of the weapon. Failure to adhere to each and every one of these criteria will result in a gun that shoots high or low, misses the target completely or has a point of impact that differs with every shot. These results are not what the shooter demands or expects, particularly when the man behind the trigger is a combat soldier and his life depends on the reliability and accuracy of his small arms.

Certainly, some technical variances must be accepted where mass-produced weapons systems are concerned, otherwise the cost of equipping an army would be utterly prohibitive. So a modern infantry rifle is expected to be accurate, but only within the accepted parameters of its intended purpose. The average soldier will not be shooting his small-calibre assault rifle at a target 1,000yds (923m) distant, but he will be required to hit a man-sized target with every shot at perhaps 300yds (274m). Thus his weapon will be designed to achieve that but little more, because more always equates to cost.

Dependable, consistent performance is doubly relevant where snipers are concerned. A sniper needs equipment that will always function reliably in extremes of heat, cold and wet, and when he is required to shoot, his rifle must work instantly and with perfect precision. It must therefore be more than just the sum of a number of factory-assembled, mass-produced parts and the care that is put into ensuring everything works, every time, naturally results in a weapon that is accurate, utterly reliable and very expensive.

For centuries the common soldier was not considered an individual, but a beast of burden who was expected to obey orders without question, fire his musket when and where ordered and who was equipped with the most basic of almost everything that the government could get away with supplying. It was not after all, until World War I that a British private soldier was actually taught to estimate range and fire at the enemy without being commanded to. Ironically, it was as a result of that conflict that the sniper began his almost glacially slow ascent from being regarded as little more than a paid assassin (a soubriquet to which they quite rightly took exception) to becoming the most highly trained and valuable of modern battlefield specialists. Where their weapons were concerned, until no more than 40 years ago it was considered perfectly acceptable for a sniper to be issued with nothing more than a standard infantry rifle onto which would be fitted a disparate mix of mounting systems and commercial optical sights, none of which were ever specifically designed for military use.

Camouflaged Russian snipers on the Eastern Front in World War II. (© The Dmitri Baltermants Collection/Corbis)

Indeed, until the 20th century the mere thought of issuing anything other than a standard military rifle to the common soldier would have had senior army officers apoplectic with indignation. Even well into the 1970s, the rationale for the existence of snipers was being seriously questioned in the British Army. They were, after all, expensive to train and generally mistrusted. Fortunately, military thinking has advanced beyond all recognition since then, in part because of the speed with which manufacturing technology has been producing extremely useful hardware. Governments can no longer ignore the inexorable march of progress, and in the 21st century armies now accept it as quite reasonable to equip a soldier with a £5,000 rifle.

But how did the musket with its 80yd (73m) range become the 1,000yd (914m) rifle, and what were the forces that drove the inventors, scientists and manufacturers to keep taking those hundreds of incremental steps forwards in the pursuit of perfection? To begin to understand the reasons, we must go back to a time where the longarm was a rarity and the concept of accuracy just a dream.

A US Marine scout/sniper, dressed in overwhites for winter camouflage, prepares to fire his M40A3 bolt-action rifle. (Corbis)

THE PURSUIT OF ACCURACY

The history of the firearm is both convoluted and incomplete. No-one knows from where exactly the first guns emerged, or when. The early handgonnes or hand-cannon, as they were called, were pot-shaped devices that fired large arrows, but they did not appear in a hand-held form in Europe until perhaps the last quarter of the 14th century. Initially these handgonnes were too heavy to fire without some form of support, but gradually they became more portable and the barrels longer and slimmer. Almost all were ignited using a burning match-cord, hence their generic name of matchlock, and gradually they became known as arquebuses. Although slow to load, their heavy 1in lead balls were deadly, delivering considerable penetrative power. Accuracy was not a prerequisite, though, with 40yds (37m) being near-maximum range for hitting a man-sized target, whereas an archer could bring down a horse at 300yds (274m) and hit a man at 100yds (91m). Moreover, a good bowman could draw and loose his arrows as fast as he could reach them, perhaps having three or four in the air simultaneously. But this skill took many years of training to master, whereas the handgonne was simple to learn, deadly at close ranges and in the early years of its use, quite terrifying to men and horses alike on the battlefield.

The blacksmiths and gunmakers who constructed these early firearms were soon looking hard at how they could improve them. The first major advance was the introduction of a mechanical lock, doing away with the simple but unreliable matchlock system. It took some experimentation, with a few false starts, but by the start of the 17th century the flintlock system had arrived, and it was to be the mainstay of armies throughout the world for over 200 years. However, while improving the method of igniting your charge was a laudable advance, it did nothing to improve the two elements that in the minds of shooters were vital for advancing the science of shooting, namely improving both accuracy and range.

There were a number of limiting factors to achieving these goals, the most serious being the commonplace use of gunpowder as a propellant. It is a low explosive and in practical terms this means that it would always seek the easiest route to escape when ignited, so putting two or three times the normal charge of gunpowder into a barrel would seldom lead to a breech explosion. It left behind a sooty, oily residue, however, which would eventually choke a barrel unless it was regularly cleaned out. It was also highly corrosive and hygroscopic, in that it would absorb moisture from the atmosphere, leading to misfires and making it almost impossible to use reliably in wet weather. Of these shortcomings, the most serious problem in achieving the holy grails of improving accuracy and range was the fouling left behind after shooting. This required the bullets, which were simple lead balls, to be manufactured in a slightly smaller diameter than the bore of the musket. By doing so the musket could be loaded even when fouled, but it also meant that the resultant gap would lead to a massive loss of propellant gas as it escaped between the ball and bore. This was known as windage, or blow-by, and it was exacerbated by the problems inherent in using spherical balls.

Round balls were aerodynamically inefficient and gyroscopically unstable, causing them to yaw in flight. Indeed, tests carried out by the author with a typical military musket of the early 19th century showed that the effective aimed range was no more than 80yds (73m) and the extreme distance at which the bullet would carry and still retain killing velocity (i.e. be capable of penetrating a human body) was about 164yds (150m), as the ball lost velocity extremely rapidly in flight. This performance issue is borne out in a textbook written in 1814 by Colonel George Hanger, an expert shot and veteran of the American Wars, who wrote that: 'A soldier's musket, if not exceedingly ill-bored ... will strike the figure of a man at 80 yards, it may even at a hundred, but a soldier must be very unfortunate indeed who shall be wounded by a common musket at 150 yards, provided his antagonist aims at him; and as to firing at a man at 200 yards ... you may just as well fire at the moon.'

In reality, few of these factors really mattered to the armies of the 18th and 19th centuries, for linear warfare was the order of the day, conducted in strict adherence to the rules of war, involving ranks of men, normally three deep, firing at the enemy just as fast as they could load. Four shots per minute were possible if each ball was dropped down the barrel and the butt pounded on the ground to seat it. At normal combat ranges, of anywhere between point-blank and perhaps 100yds (91m), actually singling out a target was quite unnecessary. Soldiers were instructed to 'present' or 'level' their arms, never to 'aim and fire', for aiming was arguably pointless and moreover it wasted time. What counted was discipline, holding your nerve in the face of a blizzard of musket balls and advancing towards the enemy with bayonets fixed when ordered to do so. It was not the best shots who normally won the day but the soldiers with the strongest nerves.

There were, however, a few methods by which windage could be eliminated. The first and simplest was the use of a patch or wad. Patches were made of many materials, thin circles of greased linen or leather being commonplace. After loading the main charge, the ball was then put onto the patch, which had been rested on the muzzle, and both were rammed down the barrel. The wad acted as a gas seal, preventing the escape of gas while helping to scour the bore clean. The resulting increase in breech pressure provided the shooter with a longer effective range and also assisted the ball in leaving the barrel with more directional stability. Proof of these results could be seen in the many shooting matches held across Europe in the 16th and 17th centuries, where accuracy was prized above all else. In Mainz, Germany, in 1547 a member of the Sharpshooters' Guild fired 20 shots at 218yds (200m), scoring 19 hits within the bullseye and one shot within 18in (46cm) of it. In America during the early years of settlement, shooting competitions were popular and there are many records of accurate shooting being accomplished at ranges of 150yds (137m), popular targets being cast-iron pans hung from tree branches.

The other method of achieving accurate shooting was far more efficient, albeit far more costly and much rarer. This was to use a system of loading the musket from the breech. Breech-loading enabled the bullet to be made exactly to the bore size of the gun; being a perfect fit there was no windage and fouling was scraped out by the passage of the close-fitting projectile. In addition, loading was much simplified – a pre-prepared charge could be used, or even a removable chamber. Such mechanisms were in use in cannon as early as the mid-14th century, and Henry VIII had no fewer than 139 such longarms in his collection in the Tower of London. Two such examples still survive, one datable to 1537. So breech-loading technology was established by the 16th century, but the ability to mass-produce such weapons was still a long way off. From around 1600 to the end of the flintlock era in the early 19th century, there were dozens of attempts to produce viable breech-loading longarms and some were tolerably successful, but the fact remained that faster loading, though of great interest to a few shooters, was of no importance to the armies of Europe. It was all very well speeding up the loading process, but doubling the range of a common musket was of interest only for sport shooting or hunting. There was only one way to reliably achieve accuracy, and that was to use rifling.

An irregular American rifleman ambushing Redcoats during the Revolutionary War. (Bridgeman)

THE RIFLED BARREL

A pair of Jäger military-pattern flintlock rifles, *c.*1750. The scrolled trigger-guard provided a firm grip and the sliding patchbox cover on the stock was typical. Unlike military smoothbores of the period both have 'V' notch rearsights and German silver blade foresights.

The potential of rifling had been glimpsed in the 15th century, when the first longarms with rifled barrels had emerged. Exactly who manufactured the first rifled barrel is unknown; like many inventions it may have occurred simultaneously in several places. But it is quite possible that the basic concept for making a projectile spin in flight was one well understood for centuries before the advent of the gun. Bowmen used arrows on which the fletchings were very slightly angled, causing the arrow to spin in flight, adding greatly to its stability and accuracy. Translating this from arrow to bullet was not a great leap of science, but actually manufacturing a rifled barrel, the inside of which must be bored with a series of spiral grooves, was no mean feat, for it had to be done with exact precision and required gunsmiths with considerable expertise. These spirals, called lands and grooves, gripped the bullet as it moved up the bore, causing it to spin and imparting gyroscopic stability. It resulted in a radical improvement in accuracy and range, enabling aimed shots to be made at 200yds (183m) and often well beyond.

One of the earliest rifling patents known is dated 1635, in which a British engineer, or possibly gunmaker, named Arnold Rotispen stated he had a process by which he could 'cutt out or screwe barrels as wyde or as close or as deep or as shallowe as shall be required'. Rotispen did not invent the process, for rifled barrels were certainly used in match rifles in Germany during the previous century, but he helped its development along, eventually leading to the perfection of the process. In 17th-century Europe the demand for these rifled guns was burgeoning. In the German states, where hunting was widespread, a form of short flintlock rifle called the *Jäger* was developed, so named after the hunters who pursued the boar, deer and wolves through the dense forests. So widespread was the use of these rifles that it aroused the interest of many of the state armies, resulting in the first models being accepted for military issue in 1711. These rifles are historically important because they were to provide the blueprint for a whole family of later rifled longarms that would be adopted across Europe and the Americas. Why they were so popular is easily explained. The design was tough, compact, with a heavy 28–33in (71–84cm) barrel with a relatively small calibre of between .52 and .65in (most military muskets were of .75–.80 calibre). They were of moderate weight, of about 8lb (3.6kg), but more importantly their accuracy was something that could barely have been dreamed of two decades earlier. Tests undertaken by the British Board of Ordnance in the late 18th century proved unequivocal:

Distance of firing (yds)	% of hits, musket	% of hits rifle
100	74.5	94.5
200	42.5	80.0
300	16.0	55.0
400	9.00	52.5

Yet despite the evidence, rifles were not regarded with any great favour by the Board of Ordnance, for several reasons. They were costly to manufacture (about double the price of a common musket) and slow to load, as the rifling grooves gradually clogged with fouling and it became increasingly hard to ram the bullets home. Unless the bore was cleaned out, it would become impossible to seat a bullet properly into the breech, with the resultant risk of an explosion on firing. Besides, the Board declared, the prosecution of modern warfare dictated no requirement for accurate longarms, although this bald assumption was soon to change in the face of some rather unruly behaviour across the Atlantic.

THE AMERICAN RIFLE

American requirements for longarms were quite different to those of Europe. Since the first settlers headed west into virgin country, the longarms they carried were vital for both protection and providing food. Many European settlers carried military-pattern muskets or commercial variants, generically known as fowling pieces. These long-barrelled smoothbore guns could be used as shotguns, loaded with small shot; as defensive weapons with a mix of larger, pistol-sized balls; or as straightforward hunting weapons, with a full-sized patched ball of around .78in.

Their shortcomings were soon obvious, though. They were too long, unwieldy, heavy, inaccurate and slow to use, particularly when settlers were confronted by hostile natives with powerful bows that could be shot with speed and accuracy from horseback. However, immigrants who had come from the Germanic states and Switzerland carried locally made rifles, with the *Jäger* type being highly popular. Russian trappers and hunters also used long-barrelled and rather elegant rifles known as *samopals*, and both of these types were greatly to influence the later design of the American rifle. There was however, no universal pattern of rifle; hunters in the plains required large-bore big-game rifles, trappers in the north preferred light, accurate rifles and settlers slowly moving westwards carried every type of variation in-between. What was clear, though, was that the old military-pattern muskets had reached the limit of their usefulness in America.

It is difficult to place an exact chronology on the gradual development of the American rifle, for different types evolved in many and varied locations over a considerable period of time. Generally speaking, however, from the early decades of the 18th century there began to appear a quite distinctive pattern of musket that owed much of its design to European

A contemporary engraving of Daniel Boone, possibly around 1770. His rifle has the scrolled trigger guard and sliding wooden patchbox cover of the German *Jäger* rifles but a much longer barrel and shows some of the early traits of the American long rifle. (Bridgeman)

heritage. Barrels became slightly shorter and slimmer with much-reduced calibres, for entirely practical reasons. A large bullet was quite unnecessary to kill either an Indian or a deer, and the smaller the bullet, the more of them could be carried for a given weight of lead. The lighter a gun the easier it was to handle and carry, vital factors when the only method of feeding oneself for weeks on end was by what could be hunted. Accuracy was more important than firepower, the very antithesis of what the military believed, and understandably demand for rifled barrels steadily increased but they were still rare. A contemporary account by an English traveller, Isaac Weld, who travelled extensively through America in the latter part of the 18th century is interesting, for he had never encountered a rifled gun before. 'The rifled barrel guns … carry leaden balls from the size of thirty to sixty to the pound [about .42 to .53in]. The inside of the barrel is fluted, and the grooves run in a spiral direction from one end of the barrel to the other, consequently when the ball comes out it has a whirling motion.'

While some rifles, particularly those made by German gunsmiths, bore a close resemblance to the traditional *Jäger*, and many thousands of longarms were still produced to military patterns, by the 1750s there had evolved a distinctive pattern of long gun that has become known, not entirely correctly, as Kentucky or Pennsylvania rifles. (The name Kentucky is actually not recorded in use prior to 1815, when a ballad called 'The Hunters of Kentucky' became widely popular.) These guns were not the preserve of any specific state or gunsmith and broadly similar types were manufactured across all of the eastern states, encompassing Philadelphia, Pennsylvania, Kentucky and Tennessee. It was a distinctive-looking arm, usually fully wood stocked, with a drooping butt that was inset with a brass patchbox and a *Jäger*-pattern scrolled brass trigger-guard. Barrel lengths were typically from 40 to 50in (102 to 127cm) and calibres varied from .40 to .55in. A 'V' type rear sight and plain blade foresight were normally fitted. It was generally accepted that such rifles were very accurate to 150yds (137m), and perfectly capable of striking a man-sized target at double that range. As the British were to find out, underestimating their capabilities would prove very costly indeed.

When fighting broke out between the colonists and British forces in 1775, initial clashes were fought on more or less traditional linear lines. As the war progressed, however, and the Redcoats ventured deeper into the vastness of the woods and forests, they became acquainted with a frightening new enemy, the American rifleman. Attempts to use riflemen as infantry early in the war proved disastrous, for they were unable to reload their rifles quickly enough and worse, could not put a bayonet on them. 'When Morgan's riflemen came down from Pennsylvania ... they marched to attack our light infantry. The moment they appeared before him he ordered his troops to charge them with the bayonet; not one in four [riflemen] had time to fire and those that did had no time to reload again ... the infantry drove them ... for miles over the country.' The riflemen soon learned, though, and soon they were being used in a more fitting role, as scouts, skirmishers and sharpshooters.

In the face of the loose ethics of modern warfare it seems odd today that the concept of deliberately targeting an enemy soldier was a completely alien one. It was widely regarded as unsporting and unmilitary, an attitude that where snipers are concerned remained until well into the 20th century. In the 18th century, men were unaccustomed to being a target and many found the experience quite unnerving. This wonderful account by a British officer during the battle of New Orleans typifies what most men thought of this new and terrifying form of warfare, and is possibly the first ever account of the psychological impact of sniper fire upon men:

> What attracted our attention most, was the figure of a tall man standing on the breastworks ... dressed in linsey-woolsey [a long woollen shirt], buckskin leggings and a broad-brimmed hat that fell around his face almost concealing his features At last he moved, threw back his hat rim, raised his rifle and took aim at our group. Our eyes were riveted on him; at whom had he levelled his piece? But the distance was so great we looked at each other and smiled. We saw the rifle flash, my right-hand companion ... fell from his saddle. The hunter paused for a few moments ... then he reloaded and resumed his former attitude. This time we did not smile. When the rifle again flashed another of our party dropped to the earth. There was something most awful in marching to this certain death. The cannon and thousands of musket balls playing upon our ranks we cared not for – for there was a chance of escaping them ... but to know that every time that rifle was levelled towards us ... to see it rest, motionless as if poised on a rack and to know when the hammer came down ... that the messenger of death drove unerringly to its goal, to know this and still march on was awful.

Just occasionally a rifleman was able to inflict a serious loss on the enemy by killing a senior officer, as evidenced when an Irish-American rifleman named Timothy Murphy shot General Simon Fraser of the 71st Highlanders. Yet despite some claims to the contrary, the use of riflemen did not materially affect the outcome of the Revolutionary Wars. They were too few in number to make a serious impact on the battlefield, but there was no doubt that those who faced them disliked the experience intensely, as one commentator wrote: 'It frequently happens that they [riflemen] find themselves run through the body by the push of a bayonet, as a rifleman is not entitled to any quarter.'

Despite their limited numbers, their appearance on a battlefield was the cause of considerable disquiet on the part of the British forces. For the first time, His Majesty's Government was moved to raise its own company of riflemen to combat them. Amateur engineer and inventor Major Patrick Ferguson had improved on a model of breech-loading rifle originally invented by the French engineer Chaumette, and in 1775 he tested it in front of officers of the Board of Ordnance, who were sufficiently impressed to order 100 of them. The company of riflemen raised were placed under the command of Ferguson and put into the field in 1776, where they proved their worth by taking on the American riflemen, and sometimes bettering them. After the battle of King's Mountain in October 1776, one surviving American commented that many of his comrades were found slumped over their rifles, 'with one eye opened in the manner of marksmen when levelling at their subjects'. But alas for posterity, Ferguson too was killed during the battle and his rifles disappeared from sight. It was however, a small portent of greater things to come.

THE 19TH-CENTURY MILITARY RIFLE

At the start of the 19th century, while Britain was still fighting the American colonists, a much more pressing problem had arisen closer to home. Napoleon Bonaparte had grand designs on Europe and it looked as though his army was coming very close to realizing his aims. In the face of the threat from across the Channel, two new regiments of British riflemen were raised, the 5/60th and 95th, but they were different soldiers in almost every respect to the common infantryman of the period. Many of the men were of a higher educational standard than normal and some were even literate. Personal intelligence was a prerequisite, for their job was to scout, skirmish and generally harass the enemy, often using their own initiative.

Skirmishing required a high level of discipline, moving forward towards the enemy with each man watching for a target while relying on his comrades to protect him from unseen threats. It was particularly dangerous in wooded country or when cavalry were about, and men were taught to fight in fours, using their shooting skills to break up threatening cavalry patrols. All recruits were expected to be excellent shots and in order for this to be achievable, the army sanctioned the first rifles ever to be supplied to British line regiments. In 1798, some 5,000 *Jäger* rifles had been ordered from Germany, but their quality was so poor that most ended up in the hands of foreign mercenaries or second-line regiments. The Board of Ordnance were generally impressed with the overall concept, though, and the design produced by London gunmaker Ezekiel Baker in 1800 was an unashamed copy of the German *Jäger* rifle, although built to a much higher standard.

With a barrel length slightly over 30in (76cm) and a bore of .70in (later reduced to .62in), the Baker rifle was strong, compact and accurate, Rifleman Harris writing that comrades of his regularly took turns at

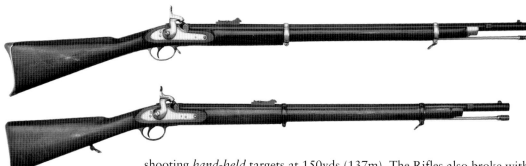

shooting *hand-held* targets at 150yds (137m). The Rifles also broke with tradition in wearing practical dark-green uniforms with black equipment and buttons, enabling them to blend with the countryside. Ambushing enemy scouting parties became something of a speciality. The French came to hate and fear them, calling them *cafards*, or grasshoppers. An unnamed French officer wrote: 'I was sent out to skirmish against some of those in green – grasshoppers I call them, you call them rifle-men. They were behind every bush and stone, and soon made sad havoc amongst my men, killing all the officers in my company, and wounding myself, without [our] being able to do them any injury.'

They were effective at longer distances, too. Private Tom Plunkett of the 95th shot General Colbert from his horse at the impressive range of 300yds (274m), an extraordinary feat. True, the Baker rifle still suffered from the drawback of slow loading, but at least it could mount a bayonet and the riflemen, when employed correctly, were usually able to provide sufficient covering fire to enable their fellows to return to the safety of their own lines.

By the end of the Napoleonic wars, the Baker rifle had found its way to most parts of the Empire, with some 40,000 having been manufactured. Indeed, the early decades of the 19th century were to prove something of a technological watershed for the rifle, for the introduction of the percussion cap in the late 1820s (which was infinitely more reliable than flint ignition) was happily coincidental with a general desire among the great powers of Europe to re-arm with modern, rifled muskets.

One of the main drawbacks of providing a large army with the latest weapons was (and still is) the cost, and so it took many years for governments around the world to adopt percussion ignition. In the case of Britain, it was in the late 1830s that the percussion musket began to appear and most of these were converted flintlocks that still retained their smooth barrels. Then, in that coincidental manner that seems to happen where technology is concerned, an invention by a French officer named Claude-Étienne Minié appeared that would change everything. It was a simple hollow conical lead bullet with a steel cup inside. As was usual, the design enabled a slightly undersized bullet to be loaded, but upon firing the skirt of the bullet expanded as the cup was pushed up into it. This gripped the rifling and the end result was vastly increased range, accuracy and power. It is no exaggeration to say that it revolutionized shooting.

LEFT
A target rifle by Marshall Tidd of New York, *c.*1854. The simple optical sight has fine elevation adjustment by screw and locknut and a windage drum. This example was used during the American Civil War, but generally they did not fare well, being too delicate for campaign service.

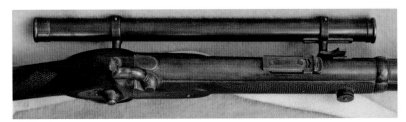

BELOW LEFT
A top view of a rare telescopic-sighted Whitworth rifle. Hugely expensive, it was only used by very small numbers of Confederate sharpshooters. The sight's rear mount is able to swivel; the front has a graduated quadrant with locking screw, providing elevation adjustment but no windage.

Militarily, no-one wanted to be left trailing behind where this new technology was concerned and within a decade it had become universally adopted (except by the United States, who remained sceptical of the design). While most armies had been supplied with percussion rifle muskets by the late 1840s, Britain was one of the last to introduce a purpose-designed weapon, but what a rifle it was, for this was the Pattern 1853 rifled musket, which set a new standard for build quality and accuracy.

Now, for the first time, British soldiers were equipped with a rifle capable of defeating a cavalry or infantry charge long before it became a physical threat. However, there lay two fundamental problems in issuing such accurate rifles to the soldiers. The first was that no-one had considered teaching the men how to use them properly, specifically with regard to range estimation. 'As the Russians came within 600 yards ... out rings a volley of Mini [Minié] musketry. The distance is too great, the Russians are not checked ... but 'ere they come within 100 yards and fifty yards, another deadly volley flashes ... they wheel about ... and fly back.' Some rudimentary teaching was given to British soldiers in how to estimate ranges. At 50yds (46m) buttons and the human face could be clearly seen; at 100yds (91m) the facial features are blurred and uniform buttons appear to be a single line. At 150yds (137m) the face is simply a white disc and uniform detail indiscernible. At 200yds (183m) only the trunk, arms and legs can be made out and the head is merely a dark blob. This was fine of course when muskets were incapable of ranges in excess of 200 yards, but the new rifles were different. The old shooting adage 'If you can't see it, you can't hit it' was never so apposite.

Nevertheless, when rifles were first issued in the final stages of the Crimean War, some British soldiers learned for themselves the value of combining careful observation and accurate shooting. Lieutenant Colonel D. Davidson (an excellent shot himself) later reported what was possibly the first example of true sniping by a pair of riflemen: 'In the rifle pits before Sebastopol … one soldier was observed lying with his rifle carefully pointed at a distant embrasure and his finger on the trigger ready to pull, while by his side lay another with a telescope directed at the same object. He … was anxiously watching the movement when the [Russian] gunner should show himself, in order that he may give the signal to fire.'

The second problem now that rifles with such potential were being issued wholesale, was how on earth did a soldier actually manage to see his enemy, when at any distance in excess of 500yds (457m), his foresight was larger than a human body?

EARLY OPTICS

In fact, the solution to the problem of long-range shooting had already been found; not as a result of the demands of the military, but by target shooters and hunters. Where the first optical sights originated is disputed. Lieutenant Colonel Davidson was a keen early advocate of optical sights and he wrote in his memoirs that he had introduced 'the telescope sight' to India for hunting use in the late 1830s. Only a tiny number of original examples of these early scoped hunting rifles exist and the few the author has seen have been fitted with long, non-adjustable telescopes mounted above the barrel, with the bore and scope collimated (zeroed) to a fixed point. As none of these rifles were in current use, the distance can only be guessed at, but using modern scope zeroing tools it would appear 100–150yds (91–137m) was an average. In many respects, the limitations of the scope defeated the long-range ability of a good rifle, but their use was primarily for hunting big game at close range.

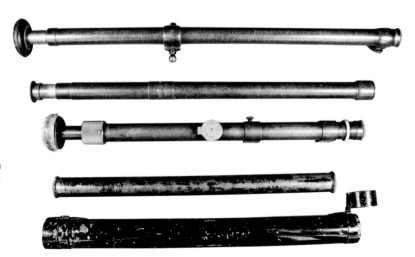

Early optical sights, from top to bottom: a Fraser with quick-release mounts, 1880; a Davidson with sliding focus c.1860; a Gibbs with sliding focus and a range drum graduated to 300yds; and an American Cataract Tool Company fixed scope of about 1902 (with its case below).

Understandably, it did not take long for shooters to begin to appreciate the benefit of using optical sights at much greater ranges. The main drawback in the early decades of the 19th century was in actually finding a source of suitable sights to use. To this end, American shooters were perhaps more fortunate, for their optical industry was expanding and they had several prominent manufacturers of high-quality glass, and that was the most vital factor. Many of these men, such as Alvan Clark and Morgan James, had learned their skills in the manufacture of telescopes and optical mirrors for stellar observation and they clearly understood the need for perfect-quality glass. Normal glass gives chromatic aberration in the form of poor focusing, a curved image and a disconcerting blue fuzzy ring around the object in view, not unlike looking through the bottom of a bottle.

The sight lens arrangements were very simple, with a pair of lenses, ocular for the end nearest the shooter and objective at the exit end of the telescope, identical to those used on ordinary telescopes. However, Clark and his contemporaries were able to produce achromatic glass, perfectly free of any imperfection. It was expensive, of course, but provided the shooter with a far sharper image and no distortion.

From the 1840s the technology became available that also permitted the manufacture of far stronger solid-drawn steel scope bodies instead of soft brass. It was an English émigré engineer named John Chapman who came up with a solution to the knotty problem of mounting the telescopes so they could be adjusted. He devised a fully adjustable set of rings with sprung internal retainers that enabled both vertical and lateral adjustments to be made. In practice, these early scopes were not easy to use, providing a very narrow field of vision of 3°–4° with low magnification, normally of 2x. These factors resulted in poor low-light performance and little target enhancement, and it made tracking a moving target extremely difficult. The length of the tubes, usually the same as or longer than that of the barrel, was also a hindrance as they were fragile and prone to being knocked out of alignment. Probably the finest exponent of this type of scope was William Malcolm of Syracuse, New York. By the late 1850s his sights were arguably the best available, which was quite fortunate for Malcolm as they became available just in time for the outbreak of the American Civil War.

The sprung ring mount pioneered by John Chapman and Morgan James. The top screw controlled elevation, the right hand, windage. Hidden by the scope tube is the spring plunger that permitted adjustment but ensured the scope body still remained firmly held in place.

THE AMERICAN CIVIL WAR SHARPSHOOTER

While Britain had ignored the concept of using rifled muskets in a sharpshooting role during the Crimean War, the Union Army was to bring the role of sharpshooter to the attention of the wider world in the momentous years of 1860–65. The American Civil War was to be fought by North and South with a curious mix of old tradition and new technology, and few of the commanders initially understood exactly how the two would change the course of warfare. Traditional mass frontal attacks by infantry were met with withering aimed rifle fire that resulted in appalling carnage, events that both sides repeated over and over again during the course of the war. Yet there were some changes made in response to this new age of firepower. Cavalry attacks, normally the scourge of the infantry, proved useless in the face of the Minié bullet and the roles of the cavalryman were redefined to those of scout and raider. For the first time, the infantry were able to inflict casualties on that most hated of battlefield specialists, the artilleryman. No longer did the hapless soldiers have to stand and impotently face shot and shell, for artillerymen foolish enough to be in view of a rifled musket could be shot at. But there also emerged a new breed of specialist, whose abilities mirrored those of the British riflemen of half a century earlier. This time, however, they appeared in far greater numbers than had ever been seen on the battlefield. They were the sharpshooters.

As we have seen, the concept of sharpshooting on the battlefield was certainly not a new one, but what the Civil War did was to organize and validate the sharpshooter. For the first time he became trained and equipped specifically to carry out his allotted tasks, and to this end the 1st Regiment of United States Sharpshooters (1st USSS) was officially

Rifleman Plunkett, the Retreat to Corunna 1808 (previous pages)

The Napoleonic rifleman was expected to be intelligent, quick-witted and above all, a good shot, and Thomas Plunkett was no exception. Of Irish birth, he joined the 95th Rifles in May 1805 and was by all accounts a model soldier, albeit with a fondness for drink. During the terrible retreat towards Corunna in the winter of 1808–09, the British forces were pressed hard by the French, and the riflemen were often used as rearguards to slow down the pursuing cavalry, who were led brilliantly by the 31-year-old General Auguste-Marie-François Colbert. If Colbert could break the rearguard he knew he would have the British Army at his mercy. By mid-afternoon on 3 January 1809, the French were crossing the river on either side of the straggling British position and Colbert rallied his men for one last effort. Breaking lines, Plunkett ran forward and, taking up the favoured back-position used for long-distance shooting, he took careful aim and shot the general dead. He then killed Colbert's trumpet-major with a second shot, before racing back to the British lines with the French at his heels. Colbert's death threw the French into confusion and allowed the British to slip away.

The Baker rifle used by the riflemen was regarded as very accurate out to 300yds, although evidence of the actual range from the battle site is not conclusive. However, from the British lines to Colbert's position varied between 200 and 600yds, so Plunkett's shots were exceptionally fine shooting regardless. Plunkett was later awarded a shilling a day pension, and died in Colchester in 1851 or 1852.

sanctioned under the command of Colonel Hiram Berdan on 15 June 1861. Unlike most existing Union regiments, which tended to be locally raised, Berdan's men were accepted from any part of the Union. As long as they proved they could shoot a 5in (12.7cm) group, offhand from 200yds (183m) then they were eligible to join. Like their Rifle regiment predecessors they were clothed in practical green uniforms, and while they were often required to perform as ordinary infantry they were given special training that infantrymen did not receive. In particular, they had to learn the specialist tasks of scouting, skirmishing and picket duties.

Skirmishing was always dangerous work, but picketing was something at which the sharpshooters excelled. John Young, a Union officer wrote: 'It is a duty that above all others ... required most individual intelligence in the soldiers.' It was a blend of guarding and scouting, relying on well-concealed forward-placed outposts. Their occupants would be the first to see and engage the enemy, targeting officers and NCOs to slow the advance. This legitimizing of shooting senior officers was also a new factor in land warfare, for no longer was it considered morally or socially unacceptable. They also had to master the difficult art of shooting at unknown ranges, and much training was given to range estimation.

Range estimation was vitally important to long-range shooting, and Union sharpshooter Major Dunlap wrote that: 'The practice was continued ... from day to day until every man could tell, almost to a mathematical certainty, the distance to any given point.' Wind estimation was also a hard skill to master, but watching grass stalks and trees could provide surprisingly accurate information. 'In a slight breeze, the grass bent just slightly, waving languidly but in a stiff wind, it bent over, often springing upright before bending down again. Very strong winds left the grasses horizontal, and unless our target was very close indeed, there was little point in attempting to execute accurate shooting.'

Colonel Hiram Berdan and California Joe, one of his sharpshooters. Joe holds a specially manufactured .52 calibre Sharps breech-loader, with double-set triggers, 2,000 of which were supplied to the two regiments of Union sharpshooters. They were arguably the first sniping rifles ever issued. (Vermont Historical Society)

A Union sharpshooter on picket duty, aiming a commercially manufactured target rifle equipped with a telescopic sight. (Bridgeman)

Berdan, himself a very talented rifle shot, was quite well aware of the need for his men to be equipped with the best available rifles. There were insufficient Enfields and besides, Berdan had already been deeply impressed with a new type of rifle that had been invented in 1858 by a brilliant engineer named Christian Sharps. Unlike its contemporaries, the Sharps rifle was a percussion (or capping) breech-loader and if there was a more suitable rifle for the regiment no-one knew of it. It was technically head and shoulders above the ordinary musket for a number of reasons. It used a pre-prepared .52-calibre combustible cartridge made with linen or paper that was fast to load and fire and with a bullet that fitted the bore perfectly. Crucially, the breech-loading mechanism meant that a soldier no longer had to stand upright and in full view of the enemy to reload; naturally, for men firing from cover this was a perfect solution. Moreover, in expert hands the Sharps was perfectly capable of being shot accurately to 1,000yds (914m) or beyond. In fact, one sharpshooter, frustrated at being unable to engage a Confederate artillery observation station, fabricated an additional rear sight ladder out of card that enabled him to shoot out to 1,500yds (1,372m). While it was not recorded that he scored any hits, the Confederates quickly decamped. Uniquely, the 2,000 rifles Berdan ordered were also fitted with double-set triggers to provide greater precision when firing, and a small number were equipped with Malcolm telescopic sights.

Adoption of the Sharps was done in the face of stiff opposition from the Army Chief of Ordnance, Brigadier General James Wolfe Ripley, who disliked breech-loading rifles, which he declared 'unnecessary'. One must have some sympathy for him, though, for a Sharps was $43 compared to $13 for a standard Springfield rifled musket and it chambered a non-standard calibre, which merely added to the already heavy logistical burden of supplying another type of bullet. In fact, the use of non-issue rifles was nothing new within the Union Army, for many men had joined up carrying their own longarms and many were of the popular heavy-barrelled (known as bull-barrelled) small-calibre type used for target shooting; a considerable number of these were equipped with optical sights. This tacit acceptance of commercial rifles for sharpshooting in warfare was to set an important precedent in America. Incidentally, the term 'sharpshooter' has nothing to do with the Sharps rifle, but is a corruption of the much earlier German word *Scharfschützen* meaning a sharp-eyed shot.

During the war, the 1st USSS proved competent in combat, and also able to provide valuable intelligence information that would otherwise have been unobtainable. So effective were they that a second regiment was formed, and of course the Confederacy was soon fielding its own sharpshooters. For ease of training, it was decided that these men would remain within their own regiments. Thus sharpshooter regiments simply became the 23rd Alabama, or 1st, 2nd, 3rd, 4th Georgia etc. In total, 16 battalions were formed.

While training was much the same as that in the North, the manual of arms drawn up by Major Calhoun Benham and Major General Cadmus Wilcox was so comprehensive that it provided the basis for much of the later sniper training in the US armed forces. What the South lacked, though, were high quality long-range rifles, as most of the weapons needed had to be smuggled through the Union naval blockade. Unlike the North, the Confederacy could not be choosy about its weapons, and standardization was something it never achieved. The best as far as the Confederacy was concerned were the imported Enfield P53 muskets. 'The superiority of the Enfield rifle for service at long range, from 600 to 900 yards, was clearly demonstrated ... while other rifles could only be relied on at a distance of 500 yards.' But although they cost $50 apiece some 117,000 were still imported.

Undoubtedly the most sought after and fabulously expensive rifle used by Southern sharpshooters was the Whitworth, and it was actually the first high-precision sniping rifle ever adopted, albeit in very small numbers. The Whitworth was manufactured in Manchester by the firm of Joseph Whitworth and was available as a basic rifle, cased with tools, or cased and fitted with accessories and optical sights. There were probably fewer than 250 Whitworths purchased and perhaps 50 of these were scoped, but as an ordinary Whitworth was $600 and a scoped example was double that, this limited acquisition is hardly surprising. Ammunition was made to exacting standards, each cartridge being dimensionally identical, with a measured charge of powder wrapped in parchment paper and lubricated with paraffin wax. In the hands of the rebels they were a deadly tool, and it was fortunate for the Union Army that the Confederates could not afford more. Union Major General Amiel Whipple was shot dead at Chancellorsville from a distance of almost 900yds (823m) and the number of senior officers who fell to sharpshooters was very great indeed. A quick tally by the author has come up with more than 30 officers *above* the rank of colonel who fell to a sharpshooter's bullet. How these killings affected the outcome of the war is impossible to calculate, but certainly both sides lost a great deal of expertise and, in some cases, irreplaceable field commanders.

The use of sharpshooters became commonplace as the war progressed, and while they were often reviled, they proved vital to both sides. Certainly their use heralded a grudging acceptance that there was some value in employing such specialists on the modern battlefield and they did affect tactics – targeting artillery units became such a speciality for sharpshooters that they forced a change in how artillery was employed. No longer could artillery units line up wheel to wheel and fire point-blank over open sights. Artillery now had to be concealed at greater distances from the front lines, and this adversely affected their performance. Of course, what no-one could calculate was the psychological effect that sharpshooters had on the ordinary soldiers, for whom a few seconds' forgetfulness could result in death and for whom relaxation was only possible when out of the firing line. The sharpshooters had brought a new, harder edge to modern warfare.

THE BOLT-ACTION AGE

At the beginning of the Civil War some infantrymen, particularly those serving in the Southern armies, had still been armed with flintlock muskets. Yet in only five years the modern breech-loading rifle had become commonplace on the battlefield. That in itself was a remarkably rapid adoption of technology, but during the war the development by Horace Smith and Daniel B. Wesson of the perfected rimfire cartridge signalled the final eradication of muzzle-loaders with their paper cartridges and separate priming. At last, there existed a self-contained metallic cartridge that was immune to rough handling, wet weather and poor storage. When used in some of the new breech-loading systems that had sprung up during the war (specifically rifles such as the Spencer and Henry), it created a perfect combination.

Boer snipers on Spion Kop, the battle for which cost the lives of 243 British soldiers. The Boers were experienced riflemen, possessing excellent knowledge of the terrain and armed with modern, accurate bolt-action rifles. (National Army Museum)

As the Civil War drew to a bloody conclusion in April 1865, its lingering legacy was an unsettling feeling among the world's most powerful armies that the march of technological innovation had, during those few turbulent years, somehow left them wanting. Centrefire cartridges had been introduced by Colonel Hiram Berdan in the United States and Colonel Henry Boxer in the UK almost simultaneously just at the close of the Civil War. By the early 1870s most countries had adopted breech-loading single-shot centrefire rifles, but the latest breed of bolt-action rifles that were appearing were technically light years ahead of these single-shot weapons.

The earliest practical bolt-action designs had appeared as early as 1841 in the form of rifles such as the Dreyse. Although single-shot, they used an immensely strong rotating locking bolt system. By the Franco-Prussian War of 1870–71, these rifles had become magazine-fed and could be fired as fast as they could be loaded. During the war there were early instances reported of sniping exchanges between both sides, but this was a case of individual shooters taking on a role rather than any organized regime.

From this time onwards, other countries naturally followed suit in acquiring bolt-action weapons, but there was still a drawback. The cartridges in use were of relatively large calibre, normally around .45in/11mm, and they required large black powder loads, with all of the problems that resulted from its use, the most inconvenient being the huge cloud of smoke emitted when firing. It was a development by French chemist Paul Vielle in 1884 that was to revolutionize ballistics. He mixed gelatinized guncotton with ether and alcohol to produce pyrocellulose (also called nitrated cellulose), which he called 'Poudre B' but is known generically today as smokeless powder. It was a remarkable chemical, for it was clean burning and produced almost no smoke on firing, would detonate only when compressed and even worked when wet. Moreover, its fast burn rate resulted in much higher velocities and greater range, so less powder was required.

The new powder inevitably led to considerable ballistic testing, the first result of which was a reduction of bullet sizes. Whereas a typical large .58-calibre lead bullet of the Civil War weighed 500 grains and would have a velocity of about 950ft/s, or 290m/s, it required a huge powder charge of perhaps 100 grains to give it long-range capability. Its conical, hollow-bodied design was not overly efficient, which meant that it lost velocity very quickly; shooters had to allow for a considerable amount of drop during its flight to compensate. But this new ammunition was different. The optimum size seemed to be about .30in/8mm and bullets were steel-jacketed with a lead core. In a landmark move in firearms history, in 1886 the French issued the Lebel rifle, the first bolt-action, high-velocity, small-calibre, smokeless powder military rifle. Without appreciating the fact, France had begun an arms race that has continued to this day. Everyone else followed suit; in 1888 Britain adopted the .303in Lee-Metford, Germany the Commission M1888 rifle, the US a .30-calibre Krag-Jorgensen, and there were dozens more – Mannlicher, Schmidt-Rubin, Mosin-Nagant, Murata, Vetterli, the list is almost endless. All used centrefire ammunition and while some, such at the Metford and Mauser, had originally been designed for black powder loads, they were soon modified to make use of the new, more powerful propellant.

The French had also realized that the typical long-bodied round-nosed bullet then commonly in use (the 'Balle M') was not efficient, despite reaching a heady 2,000ft/s (610m/s), for its long-range performance was disappointing. In late 1898, they adopted the 'Balle D', a sharply pointed, solid-machined brass bullet with a slightly tapered tail. Its velocity was a useful 2,400ft/s (732m/s) but more importantly the bullet design gave it a flatter trajectory and more stable flight. In 1905 Germany adopted the S-Patrone, with a similar bullet design which they designated 'spitzer' or pointed, but with a much improved 2,800ft/s (853m/s) performance, and Britain changed from the old round-nosed Mk VI cartridge to the .303in Mk VII spitzer in 1910. Most of the world was by now armed with rifles of near-identical type, function and performance. In the event of war it should have been a level playing field where rifles were concerned, but events in South Africa proved otherwise.

Although not a world war by any standards, the Boer campaigns of 1880–81 and 1899–1900 were to prove that an untrained, disparate group of farmers who were poorly equipped but highly motivated and mobile could outfight and outshoot Queen Victoria's finest. Small mounted Boer units, known as *kommandos*, began a series of hit-and-run raids and ambushes on British troops, and what impressed the British above all else was the terrible accuracy of the Boer riflemen. Unlike other colonial campaigns, the British faced men who had keen eyesight, a deep knowledge of the landscape and how to utilize its natural camouflage – and the best rifles they could get. Favourites were M1896 Mausers, as well as captured Lee-Enfields and Metfords, Krag-Jorgensens and Mannlichers, in fact almost any modern weapon that was available commercially.

Initially the British soldiers took little advantage of cover, believing not unreasonably that if they couldn't see the enemy, they were safe. Lieutenant F. M. Crum wrote: 'I counted some 500 ponies and many Boers. What was the range? Major Greville thought it was 1,200 yards, I put it at more. We called for a rangefinder, but it had been left behind.' Just how effective their shooting was became evident in the battle for Spion Kop on 23–24 January 1900. When attacking British troops failed to reach the summit of the 1,400ft (430m) hill, they took refuge in a depression a little below it. The Boers, surrounding them on three sides, were able to fire into the British positions at ranges from 500 to 1,000yds (457 to 914m), and they killed 243 British soldiers for the loss of 68 of their own, mostly as a result of artillery fire. Many officers and soldiers who suffered at the hands of Boer riflemen never forgot the experience, and little more than a decade after this demonstration of the power of the marksman, the sniper would reappear, this time in a very different conflict.

WORLD WAR I

GERMAN RIFLES

Few senior officers on the Allied side believed the conflict that began in August 1914 would last beyond three or four months, the expected result being the Germans driven from French soil by the combined efforts of the Allied armies. No-one envisaged the establishment of a trench system running nearly 450 miles (725km) from the Belgian coast to the Swiss border. Of all the combatant powers, it was only Germany that had the foresight to plan for the eventuality of a static war, and to this end they had begun before 1914 to acquire rifles for use by trained *Scharfschützen*, or sharpshooters.

Obtaining rifles was facilitated by the fact that in 1913 Germany and Austria were producing more optically equipped hunting rifles than the combined output of the rest of the world. The hunting of large game such as deer, boar and wolf had always been a major social event in Germany and target shooting was also a well-established pastime. There was also the militaristic nature of Germany society that required voluntary army service from its young men, who regarded joining the army as an honour rather than a chore. This provided Germany with a core of good marksmen who were often absorbed into *Jäger* battalions, somewhat akin to the British Rifle regiments.

Upon the outbreak of war, there were in excess of 15,000 scoped rifles in private hands in Germany and the government wasted no time in requisitioning them for military use. Indeed, if you owned one, it was a civil offence not to surrender it to your local town hall. The shortcoming of many of these rifles was their fragility, for they were never designed for the rigours of trench warfare. Additionally, most had been manufactured pre-war to chamber the old Patrone-88 hunting cartridge and they would not function safely with the more powerful 7.92mm spitzer military ammunition. Many had metal plates attached to them stating: 'Nur fur Patrone-88, Keine S-Munition Verwenden' (Only to be used with 8mm ammunition, unsuitable for S-ammunition).

But for Germany, the use of such weapons was merely an interim measure, as production was well underway of a dedicated sniping rifle, the Scharfschützen Gewehr 98. The standard Mauser infantry rifle, the Gewehr Modell 1898 (Gew 98), was an extremely robust design with an almost unbreakable three-lug bolt-locking system, five-shot internal magazine and a receiver that lent itself easily to the mounting of bases for telescopic sights. Its general performance was excellent and selected Gew 98s were taken from the production lines for conversion to sniping rifles. These weapons proved to be exceptionally accurate when test fired, being capable of 1in (25mm) five-shot groups at 91yds (100m). Individual rifles were then converted by armourers, many of whom had been peacetime gunsmiths. Each was stripped and a set of mounts, rings and a telescope were allocated to the weapon. The rings and scope were carefully soldered together in a jig, to ensure the scope body was perfectly horizontal, and the mounts were loosely attached to the body of the rifle. The rings and scope were then mounted on the rifle and collimated (or aligned) with the bore. Any error at this stage could result in a rifle that would never shoot accurately. When satisfied that this was as near perfect as could be achieved, the bases were properly fitted to the action, usually by both screwing and soldering. Quite often some hand fitting of the claw mounts was needed to achieve a perfect fit and in total this work would normally occupy one armourer for a week. The standard of workmanship on these rifles was equal to that on commercial rifles, for the work was done by craftsmen.

German sniper in a trench on the Western Front during World War I. (Mary Evans/Robert Hunt Collection)

Crucially, Germany also had access to the finest selection of optics then available, from the Austrian Schott Glaswerke, established in Jena in 1884. Schott had perfected the art of manufacturing very high-quality optical glass on a large scale and as a result there were manufacturers such as Zeiss, Voigtlander, Gerard, Busch and others who offered the discerning shooter a wide range of optical sights. The design of these had been vastly improved since the introduction of the early American tube types, particularly in respect of the lens arrangement. No longer was a pair of lenses used, but instead multiple groups with additional centre-mounted erector and collective lenses were installed – up to six individual lenses. This increased magnification to 3x, 4x or greater, while enlarging the objective lenses provided the shooter with a much brighter and larger image, as well as greatly enhancing the low-light capability of the scope. (The larger the objective lens, the greater the amount of light that entered it.) Some telescopes were fixed focus, others had a focal adjusting ring, but all benefited from having an external elevation drum fitted. Neither did the shooter have to rely on fragile external mounts for adjustment, for these second-generation scopes had internal crosshairs (or reticules) that could be moved up and down by turning a drum on top of the scope body, to adjust the range. Each scope was tested and the graduations then marked on top of the range drum, in increments of 100m, up to 800m or occasionally 1,000m.

The much stronger telescope designs alleviated the problems of mounting the scope to the rifle, for fixed mounts were used that were extremely tough and unaffected by normal handling. German gunsmiths knew that for the best possible accuracy fitting the scope above the barrel was by far the most efficient method, and by the turn of the century most hunting rifles had overbore mounts that were screwed and soldered to the top of the breech (on the flat surface called the knox-form) and to the rear of the bolt housing.

A double-claw mount scope set-up by Otto Bock, on a Mauser Gew 98 rifle. The rear mount is curved to permit use of the iron sights. The small square stud visible on it was for windage adjustment.

31

Although there were dozens of variations of scope and mounts they fell into two main types: overbore and partially offset. Overbore required the scope to be mounted in a direct line of sight over the barrel and the mounts were usually bridged. Offset used mounts that were fitted to the left of the action and curved to the right, still placing the scope in line with the bore. Both systems permitted use of the iron sights.

This work was based on practical experience gained pre-war in the fabrication of hunting rifles and it proved to be both durable and effective. There was particular practical importance to using the overbore mounting system, for the German Army was plentifully supplied with steel loophole plates from which to observe and snipe. Rifles with offset scopes simply did not work well with loopholes, as the British were to find out. Usually these steel mounts were bridged or curved, which enabled the shooter to use the rifle's iron sights for close-range shooting.

The rings into which the scope was soldered or clamped had claw mounts that locked into slots in the mounting brackets on the rifle, providing a quick-release system that in theory did not require the scope to be re-zeroed if removed. It was simple, strong and soldier-proof – indeed, the claw-mounting system was so strong that a rifle could be picked up by the body of the scope without altering its zero, something that was never possible with the old telescopic sights. One problem remained, though, which was how to adjust for lateral movement (windage – see Glossary) of the bullet caused by side-winds, when the scope was in a rigidly fixed mount. This was dealt with by building into the rear mount of the scope a threaded screw that, when turned with a small key, moved the scope body fractionally left or right, but it was fine adjustments only.

BRITISH RIFLES

Thus when war broke out, British and French troops found themselves under inexplicably accurate rifle fire, which was initially attributed to the number of good shots in the German Army, but as trench warfare became universal, the problem persisted. One officer noted: 'We lost men at a steady and depressingly regular rate while in Plugstreet. The slightest movement above the parapet drew immediate fire from the Germans and in one day the battalion lost twelve men, all head shots from which there was no recovery.'

Because no provision had been made for fighting a large-scale war, or equipping specialist troops such as snipers, Britain and the Commonwealth lagged far behind in the supply of rifles and optical sights. A few were available commercially from larger gunsmiths and many found their way into the front lines in late 1914 and early 1915. Most of these were big-game hunting weapons by Rigby, Purdey, Jeffery and others and were of non-standard calibres, .333, .450, .500 and even .600in, and surviving papers show 62 such rifles were purchased by the government for frontline issue. While they were excellent for smashing through the German sniper plates (something a standard .303in bullet could not do), their recoil made them difficult to shoot from a prone position and they were not well suited to the rigours of trench life.

In the face of the enormous level of sniping from which the Allied armies were suffering, it was clear that some response had to be made. Luckily there were a few experienced and competent officers, such as F. M. Crum, who had had experience of being on the receiving end of sniper fire during the Boer War, and others like Vernon Hesketh-Prichard and Neville Armstrong who were highly experienced big game and target shooters. Between them, they bullied and cajoled the army command to instigate a sniper training programme and, more importantly, sanction the building and issue of a sniping rifle. To this end the army was in something of a dilemma, for the most suitable rifle, the excellent Enfield Pattern 1914, was not in large-scale production, having been sidelined because its original calibre of .276in had caused reliability problems. Re-tooling to manufacture it in .303 calibre would have been slow and expensive. Instead the Mk III Short, Magazine Lee-Enfield (SMLE) was to be the rifle of choice. While it was an excellent all-round battle rifle, being compact and well built, it was not designed with long-range accurate shooting in mind. This could be achieved, of course, by using a heavier barrel and very high-quality commercial ammunition, but in a wartime economy this was hardly practical. It did possess advantages over the Mauser, however, being shorter, with a faster-operating cranked bolt-handle, finer trigger action and ten-round magazine. In standard form it was reasonably accurate out to 600yds (550m) with issue ball ammunition. A swift decision was needed, so the SMLE was selected for sniper conversion.

An early attempt at producing a British sniping rifle, using a French APx MIle 1915 scope mounted to an Mk III Lee-Enfield. The beautiful quality of workmanship hints at one of the best London gunmakers, Purdey, Churchill or similar.

A major problem facing the British Army was finding sufficient optical sights for the rifles, for there was a limited availability of telescopic sights in England – most optical glass was being used for artillery gunsights, telescopes and binoculars. Neither was there any single accepted pattern of mounting sights on rifles; most of the big gunmakers, like Jeffery, Rigby and Purdey, produced their own variations on a theme. Some British sniping rifles were even fitted with German and French telescopic sights, while others used British-manufactured scopes such as Watts or Evans. Indeed, the full extent of this experimentation is still being uncovered by firearms historians, but after hurried negotiations in May 1915 a document called 'Specification 390' was drawn up and issued to potential contractors.

The actual number of contractors and types of mounts supplied is uncertain today, but there were three primary patterns issued for service. Most numerous were the scopes produced by the Periscopic Prism Company (PPCo) of Kentish Town. They were physically big sights at 12in (7.2cm) long and weighed almost 1lb 8oz (0.7kg), but had only 2x magnification, which was a problem for longer-distance shooting as sniper Private J. Huxford later recalled. 'I had a PPCo scope on my rifle... They were not good at long ranges though, the magnification was not powerful enough and I shot mostly between one hundred and four hundred yards, besides the offset was very difficult to use.' The scope was a robust design, however, that could be adapted to any number of different mounting systems, and some 4,836 PPCo mounted rifles were produced.

A rare photo of snipers of the King's Own Regiment on Salonika, possibly June 1916. The nearest soldier holds an SMLE with PPCo scope. Rifles number one and three, sitting on the wall to his right, are fitted with Galiean sights, the large glass objective lenses just being visible. The last but one man in the trench is peering through an artillery rangefinder. (Imperial War Museum CO36)

Second was a telescope produced by Birmingham's well-established Aldis company. It started off as the Aldis No.1, a 2.5x instrument, but through development eventually became the Aldis No.4, 3x variant. Some 3,196 were issued and fitted not only to SMLEs, but also later P14 rifles. The third most prolific was an American commercial telescope manufactured by Bausch and Lomb for Winchester, the A5. This was a design than harked back to the late 19th century, being a slim tube design that had no inbuilt elevation or windage adjustment. It relied on the old method of ring mounts for adjustment, which were easy to use and very precise but delicate and prone to accidental damage. Yet it was usefully of 5x power and was well liked by those who used it. Herbert McBride, a Canadian sniper and author, wrote that: 'Men returning from a sniping course … are convinced that the Winchester sight is the best for practical work.'

For all Commonwealth snipers, the biggest single drawback to the telescopic sights fitted to the Enfield rifles were that they were offset to the left. This location made finding a comfortable shooting position difficult, as Private Huxford commented. 'These telescopes took some getting used to and while we were taught to shoot using the right eye it was difficult to get a comfortable position. Later … I learned to shoot left-eyed but I used to wrap a field dressing around the stock to have a decent rest for my cheek.' More seriously, it rendered the steel loophole plates nearly useless as the narrow aperture blocked vision, particularly if the rifle was angled to the right. To counter this problem, some British plates had a larger firing slit, but this compromised them as German snipers could shoot through it. The problem vexed all Allied snipers, and was never satisfactorily solved during the war.

AMMUNITION

The accuracy of these rifles allied to the high velocity of the bullets (around 2,850ft/s or 869m/s for a 7.92mm) meant that even a sandbag parapet 2ft thick was little protection from a bullet fired from close range. Most trench sniping was done from under 300yds (274m) and a standard ball round could punch through two courses of bricks, 6in (15cm) of hard timber or 4ft 6in (1.4m) of piled earth. Hardly any soldiers had experience of being under fire from such projectiles and the wounds caused were shocking to them. Lieutenant Hesketh-Prichard recalled men falling with head wounds: 'The hardiest soldier turned sick when he saw the effect of the pointed German bullet which was apt to keyhole so that a little hole in the forehead … became a huge tear the size of a man's fist on the other side.' The myth soon grew up in the British Expeditionary Force that the Germans routinely used dum-dum or tampered bullets to cause more frightful wounds. So strong was this belief that many soldiers, in spite of the Geneva Convention forbidding it, made their own, as Private Frank Richards recalled. 'We could always tell when a man had been hit by an expanding bullet, which caused a frightful wound. Whenever one of our men got shot by one of these bullets some of us would cut the tips off our own bullets … and then go on sniping with them.' In reality, altering these bullets in any manner at all would have been counter-productive, for it would seriously compromise their accuracy at anything other than near point-blank range, and no sniper would touch anything other than a proper factory-supplied cartridge.

There was an exception to this rule, though, for it had been discovered by the Germans that if a bullet was reversed in its cartridge and fired at a steel plate, it would penetrate it. In effect, it acted as a sabot round, the jacket of the bullet stopping suddenly while propelling the core through the metal. It was of no use for ranges greater than 100yds or so, but very effective nevertheless. In spring 1915, Germany became the first country to issue armour-piercing ammunition for any purpose other than aircraft use, and it provided snipers with specific instructions as to its use in Gew 98 rifles.

Commonwealth snipers train at one of the frontline sniper schools in France. The officer standing at centre holds an SMLE fitted with a German prismatic scope.

Every batch of ammunition, regardless of where it was made, was marked up with a lot or batch number as it was packed and as long as these numbers were the same, every cartridge should have performed in exactly the same manner as the first. If a different lot number was used, however, the rifle had to be re-zeroed as the bullet performance was usually fractionally different, as Canadian sniper C.W. Newman of the 2nd Mounted Rifles noted. 'We tried very hard in the sniper section to keep a big supply of the same brand and batch of ammunition which saved having to zero our rifles. This was a slow process as the lateral adjustment on the PP [Periscopic Prism Co.] scopes was very troublesome. There was a lot of grousing when we were issued new ammunition for we all had to leave the line to reset our rifles and sights.'

ALLIED RIFLES

The Commonwealth forces all used scoped variants of the SMLE, although in 1915 Canadian troops had arrived in France with the .303in straight-pull Ross rifle fitted with the clumsy American-designed 5x Warner & Swasey scope. This was a prismatic scope that uniquely had both adjustable range and elevation drums on the mount body, but it suffered from loss of zero if roughly handled and the scope was notorious for the closeness of its ocular lens to the firer's eye, often resulting in bad bruising and uncontrollable flinching. In practice, the Ross proved too delicate for trench warfare and was withdrawn in 1916, with only a few remaining as sniping rifles.

America, too, was suffering a degree of confusion about what should be issued for sharpshooting and sniping, and the Army had also settled on the Warner, but fitted to the .30-calibre Springfield M1903 rifle. It was a tolerably good combination, but the Marines disliked it and ordered a new design M1918 scope manufactured by Winchester, although the war was to end before any significant numbers were issued. Nevertheless, many

TOP
A US Marine Springfield Model 1903, with Winchester A5 scope, that saw service during World War I. The remains of the sniper's padded cheek piece can be seen on the stock.

BOTTOM
The much-maligned Ross rifle, with Warner & Swasey scope. The fore-end has been cut down to aid accuracy by preventing the wood touching the barrel. When used with good-quality ammunition and kept clean, the Ross was actually a very competent sniping weapon.

American riflemen proved themselves extremely competent snipers using only iron sights, with which they were quite capable of accurate shooting at ranges well beyond that of most scope-equipped rifles. Private Herman Davis of the 113th Infantry Battalion, having been told that at 1,000yds a German machine-gun was beyond practical rifle range, commented dryly, 'Thet's jest a good shootin' distance' before despatching all four of the gun team.

It was not only the British who suffered from a lack of suitable sniping tools, for France had little in the way of sniping equipment and was forced to modify the 8mm Lebel rifle, a wholly unsuitable 19th-century design, into a sniping role. Fortunately, there existed a good optical industry, mostly based around Paris, and the excellent Atelier de Puteaux workshops produced a quite effective telescope loosely based on an existing model used for a light field gun. It was a 3x design that was very similar to the German Gerard and was issued as the A.Px Mlle 1915. It went through several variants and was also fitted to the Berthier rifle. How many A.Px telescopes were manufactured is unknown, but probably fewer than 5,000.

As the war progressed, the British and Commonwealth forces instigated a training schedule for snipers at a number of schools along the Western Front and in the UK, whose content was to form the basis of most British sniper training up to the 21st century. As regards the wartime performance of the rifles and scopes, they worked tolerably well in the prevailing conditions, but their long-range shooting ability was limited in part by the available optics and by the quality of barrels, which were thin-walled and lost their accuracy after about 500 rounds. In addition, the use of standard-issue military ball ammunition, which was made to less-than-exacting wartime standards, did not aid accuracy. In practice this issue probably didn't matter overmuch, for as Hesketh-Prichard, the pre-eminent master of British sniping, wrote: 'If there was any wind at all, shooting at any range beyond 400 yards was a waste of ammunition.' Certainly the excellent optics fitted to German rifles and the use of overbore mounts made them more practical and many argued that the long-barrelled Mauser was a better sniping rifle for longer ranges, but the Enfield coped adequately in a role for which it was never designed. At the end of the war, all this counted for little, as expenditure was slashed and the armies of the world shrank back to peacetime levels. No-one wanted the expense of retaining and training snipers, and the skills learned faded along with the veterans. But the cuts were eventually to prove to be a false economy.

WORLD WAR II

In the latter stages of World War I there had been a gradual realization that the Mk III Enfield did not perform well in a sniping role. Ironically there had been a replacement waiting in the wings since before the war, in the shape of the Enfield Pattern 1914, but the inability of Great Britain to manufacture it meant that most examples had been made under contract in America by Winchester. It was based very closely on the Mauser, using the same bolt locking system, and was an extremely accurate rifle. During late 1916, some began arriving at the School of Musketry at Hythe in Kent and a number found their way into the sniper training schools, where they proved exceptionally good. This performance was in part because they were fitted with an excellent micro-adjustable ladder rear sight that many snipers thought to be as good as, if not superior to the available optical sights.

It was decided that a proper sniping variant, the Pattern 1914 Mk I W (T), should be trialled. Even the scope mounts were copied from existing German rifles, for the rifle used a double claw at the front and quick-release single claw at the rear. Aldis scopes were fitted, although a few examples with PPCo scopes are known. Crucially, all scopes were mounted overbore, eliminating all of the earlier problems with offset mounts. Unfortunately, the rifle was not officially approved for production until December 1918, by which time the war had ended. Of the 11,798 existing scoped rifles, some 9,788 were stripped of their optics, which were sold into the commercial gun trade and the rifles stored, or sold to Commonwealth countries.

Elsewhere around the world, the situation was little better. Germany was forced to severely limit the size of its army and only a tiny proportion of sniping rifles remained in military hands; probably more were kept in private houses by returning soldiers than were ever returned to their armouries. Most French Lebel and Berthier rifles that had been scoped were also stripped of their optical sights then sold off to African colonies. A Canadian government survey in 1923 showed fewer than 250 complete

scoped rifles were held in store. The US Army had never really instigated a proper sniper training scheme and while some Marine Springfield rifles had been fitted with scopes late in the war, it was too little, too late. The Marines did continue with a high standard of rifle shooting, though, fielding many successful shooting teams through the post-war years, but no real decision was made concerning the manufacture of a dedicated rifle for sniping.

SOVIET SNIPER RIFLES

Few governments were concerned at this state of affairs, except perhaps Russia who, paradoxically, had not possessed any snipers at all during the Great War. Its soldiers had suffered grievously at the hands of Austrian and German snipers and the newly appointed Soviet military commanders were not about to let the situation be repeated. Fortunately, post-war Russia had purchased the Zeiss factory in eastern Germany, which gave it access to the latest designs as well as excellent optical glass. So in the early 1930s, the ubiquitous Mosin-Nagant M1891/30 rifle was matched to the excellent PEM scope based on German Zeiss-Jena and Emil Busch models. Although the Nazi regime eventually removed the factory from Russian control in 1938, it had by then produced some 54,160 PEM scopes.

The PEM was just over 10in (25.4cm) long, with 4x magnification and had built-in elevation and windage drums, making adjustment quick and easy. Several hundred were issued to Soviet forces fighting in the Spanish Civil War and they proved robust and accurate. Mounts were conventional, the PEM having a 'U' bracket mounted on the left side of the receiver, attached by two large thumb screws. In the mid-1930s a more compact version, the 3.5x power PU, was produced. It provided a useful 4° field of view, was a mere 6½in (16.5cm) long and was graduated from 100 to 1,300yds. It was to become the most widely issued optical sight ever manufactured, more than 100,000 being made to 1945 and as many again up to 1958, when production ceased, and it provided the blueprint for a new generation of similar scopes. It had an unusual T-shaped mounting bracket, held in place by a stud at the front and very large thumb screw at the rear, with two locking screws. Theoretically, removal of the scope and mount would not affect zero, but few snipers were prepared to remove it unless absolutely necessary. Much depended on the quality of ammunition, but generally, accuracy of a good Mosin-Nagant M1891/30 was a little over one minute of angle (1 moa), which equated to 1in (2.54cm) at 100yds (91m), 2in (5cm) at 200yds (184m) and so forth. As a human head is about 8in (20.3cm) wide by 11in (27.9cm) tall, this accuracy enabled a head shot to be taken at 500yds (457m) and a chest shot at 800yds (732m).

In late 1939, Russia invaded Finland and began fighting a winter war against the Finns in which it would receive a salutory lesson. Coincidentally, the Finnish Army also used the same Mosin-Nagant, and Finnish snipers proved a nightmare for the inexperienced Russians, the snipers infiltrating the Soviet lines, killing and departing, leaving no trace. Many were professional hunters, used to the bitter conditions, well clothed and very hardy. Although scoped rifles were available, most preferred to shoot with open sights as the fierce cold, often -58°F (-50°C), froze scope drums and frosted lenses. Their highest-scoring sniper, Simo Häyhä, achieved 542 *confirmed* kills using only open sights. (His actual total, adding in unwitnessed kills, is possibly double that figure.)

The experience was a sharp wake-up call for the Soviets, who lost in the region of 500,000 men during the year-long campaign, and as a result Red Army tactical doctrine regarding the use of snipers was re-evaluated. When Nazi forces rolled into the Soviet Union in 1941, they were to meet head-on the best equipped and trained sniping force in the world. The Soviet Army possessed in excess of 100,000 telescope-equipped rifles at the beginning of the war, and the PE- or PU-equipped Mosin-Nagants were basic, strong, easily repaired and performed well in the appalling weather conditions of Soviet winters.

But there were limitations with using a bolt-action rifle in firefights. Increasingly, combat became confined to fighting in built-up areas, small combat teams stalking each other through the ruins of Soviet cities and their rabbit warrens of cellars and drains. Single-shot rifles were slow to use, and while both sides issued huge numbers of submachine guns, there was clearly a need for a semi-automatic infantry rifle with greater accuracy and penetration than a submachine gun as well as the capability to mount a scope for sniping. The Russians had taken the lead prior to the Finnish War

A Soviet sniper with Mosin rifle and PEM scope explains his technique to admiring local women. (From the fonds of the RGAKFD at Krasnogorsk via Nik Cornish)

The 3.5x Soviet PU scope, mounted here on an SVT40 semi-automatic sniping rifle. With its large and simple to operate range and windage drums it was a revolution in telescopic sight design and was soon copied by Germany. The rifles proved to be competent but not outstanding sniping weapons.

when they introduced the flawed Tokarev SVT38 (Samozaryadnaya Vintovka Tokareva; Tokarev Self-Loading Rifle) based on a Simonov design from 1936. It chambered the Soviet 7.62mm cartridge and used a gas-recoil system that operated a piston in a gas tube above the barrel. Upon firing, a gas take-off port in the barrel channelled waste gas into the tube, blowing back the piston and cocking the rifle. As a design it was clever and it was to be copied in many guises later on. As an infantry rifle, however, it proved too unreliable, with a heavy recoil, parts failures and tendency to jam through ingress of mud and dirt. Nevertheless, a number were fitted with scopes and when kept in a well-maintained condition they showed some promise.

In 1940, the SVT38 was modified and re-introduced as the SVT40. The SVT40 used the short PU scope with a clever tuning-fork-shaped mounting bracket that slid into rails on the rear of the receiver. It proved to be a competent but not outstanding sniping rifle, with an effective range of about 650yds (600m). Its main virtue lay in its rapid-fire capability, as reported by sniper Vassili Zaitsev:

> We lay in our stakeout in the ruins of a little house. The Germans were marching in formation. We allowed them to approach to about three hundred metres away … and then we began to shoot. There were about one hundred of the Germans. One man fell, then another, then another … it takes two seconds to take a shot and the SVT rifle has a ten-round magazine. We killed forty-six Germans there. That is how important the sniper's role was in the defence of Stalingrad.

It was to be the first in a long line of semi-automatic sniper rifles that would be used in the Soviet Union, the descendants of which are still in military service. Most sniping on the Eastern Front was brutal and unglamorous, with captured snipers routinely being tortured to death, and it bore little resemblance to the Hollywood image so recently portrayed.

Female Soviet snipers wearing the loose two-piece 'amoeba' camouflage suits widely issued on the Eastern Front. (Courtesy of the Central Museum of the Armed Forces, Moscow, via Nik Cornish)

GERMAN SNIPER RIFLES

At the beginning of the war, little consideration had been given to producing a standard sniping rifle. Germany had adopted the short-barrelled version of the Gew 98, the K98k, before the end of World War I, and by 1939 it was the standard for all infantry use. Some SS units were equipped with early K98k rifles converted to sniping use with the addition of a short side-rail scope mount. Army units fielded a mixture of World War I-surplus Gew 98s, many modified to the shorter K98k pattern and fitted with an ad hoc mixture of scopes and mounting systems.

In the wake of the invasion of the USSR, calls began for the rapid acquisition of proper sniping rifles, so Germany embarked on the production of a bewildering number of models and types; short side-rail, long side-rail, turret mount, claw mount, SS double claw mount, Gew 43 side-rail, plus several scope mounts for the new breed of assault rifles, the FG42 and MP43/44, neither of which were ever conceived with a view to sniping. Captured Russian rifles were routinely used and Soviet scopes sometimes grafted onto Mauser rifles.

The most commonly issued sniping rifle to the Wehrmacht during World War II was this Mauser K98k/High Turret combination. It was not much different to the set-up of the previous war, but the scopes were of slightly higher magnification and the size of the objective lens was greatly enlarged.

43

Germany wasted little time in producing its own version of the Russian scope, this example being a ZF4. It had a quick-release sliding mount that unlatched with a simple thumb-catch, but was prone to accidental release. Like the Tokarevs, the semi-auto Mauser G43 rifles were not accurate at long ranges, but their firepower was immensely useful in close combat.

The number of variants of German optical scopes used was legion. Many early rifles were fitted with commercial telescopes of Great War design, being 3x or 4x, graduated to 1,000m and having only an elevation drum, windage being by use of the usual rear turn-screw. In an attempt to move away from the time-consuming hand fitting of scopes to rifles, a sharpshooter's rifle, the Zeilfernrohr 41, was produced in 1941 with a tiny 1.5x optical sight. Hitler decreed that 6 per cent of all production rifles would be so equipped and some 370,000 sights were scheduled for production by 15 different makers. These rifles had a special dovetail rail mounted on the left of the rear sight base, so the scope could be quickly removed. In practice it was a compromise that satisfied no-one. The incredibly long eye relief provided a tiny field of view of about 2°, which made tracking even a barely moving target almost impossible – iron sights were more effective. The low power gave no distance visibility and lenses misted up easily, and adjustment for zeroing was also time-consuming, requiring special tools. Probably fewer than 100,000 were actually produced. However, this figure still makes it the largest production of a German telescopic sight, and it was a precursor to the modern concept of fitting image-enhancing optical sights on assault rifles.

A German sniper waits in a treetop. Trees were a poor choice for a hide, for once a sniper was spotted he was doomed. (Bundesarchiv)

Naturally Germany followed the Russians in producing a semi-automatic rifle, introducing two variants on the SVT; one was designed by Louis Schmeisser, the other by Karl Walther. The Walther proved to be the preferred model, but when introduced as the Gewehr 41, it proved troublesome, particularly the complex design of gas-cup arrangement around the barrel that was required to cycle the action. In the wake of strident calls for improvements it was modified and became the 7.92mm Gew 43. This rifle utilized a more conventional gas take-off system from the barrel and proved to be a sound weapon. For sniping use a simple thumb-activated quick-release side-rail mounting system was attached to the right side of the receiver for mounting the ZF4 scope. The ZF4 was itself something of a landmark design, for it was manufactured using a casting process that kept weight down. Similar to the PU, it was very compact and equipped with windage and elevation drums. Some had ranging crosshairs fitted instead of the normal crosshair and post, and late in the war a few were fitted to modified mounts on K98k rifles. Each branch of the German military wanted their own dedicated sniper rifles, so by the end of the war there were ten production models in use and several other experimental variants. It was hugely wasteful in terms of design and manufacturing costs, and was certainly not the way that Britain intended to do things.

This tiny ZF-41 scope was produced in larger numbers than any other German scope of World War II and was important in being the first attempt at providing the ordinary infantryman with an enhanced optical sight that could be fitted to a standard rifle. In practice it was fiddly to adjust, difficult to use and vulnerable to damage.

COMMONWEALTH SNIPER RIFLES

The armed forces of Britain and its Commonwealth allies were in a parlous state when war broke out. Cuts in military funding had reduced the British Army to a shadow of its former self, and the situation was no better where weapons were concerned. In 1939 there was no standard sniping rifle available, although some 10,000 ordinary Enfield Pattern 1914 rifles were held in stores. The company of Alex Martin of Glasgow were contracted to fit Aldis and some PPCo telescopic sights to them, so in the region of 800 were converted to become No.3 Mk I*(T) A rifles. Good as they were, the scopes and mounts were Great War designs and the rifle itself no longer in production.

Fortunately, the post-war British government had decided to continue with its plan to upgrade the old Mk III SMLE, and after ten years of trials, the No.4 Mk I rifle was adopted in November 1939. Apart from an aperture rear sight, exposed muzzle and protected foresight, it was in most other respects similar to the Mk III, even having the same five-groove, 1:10 left-hand twist rifling of the SMLE. (The twist is the ratio of turn that the bullet makes in the barrel; 1:10 equates to one turn in 10in, and the ratio affects the stability of the bullet in flight.) But it was clear that the available sniping rifles were insufficient to meet what was going to be a long, hard war, so almost immediately as the No.4 Mk I was adopted, trials began to produce a sniper variant.

The design team at Enfield were materially assisted by the existence of a telescope, the No.32 Mk I, which had been primarily designed for use with the Bren light machine-gun. It was never issued, for the demands of wartime production made this impossible, but the telescope proved ideal for use with the No.4. It was a large, solid instrument, weighing 2lb 5oz (1.1kg) with its mount, with 3x magnification and 9° field of view. It was fitted with the normal pointer and crosswire crosshairs. Range and windage drums gave 2 moa adjustment (2in per 100yds) but later models had a finer 1 moa drum fitted and elevation could be adjusted to 1,000yds (914m). The cast-iron mounting bracket, attached to the left of the receiver with two large thumb screws, was believed by most snipers to be unbreakable, one remarking that if cornered he could remove his scope and mount and beat the Germans to death with it.

From May 1940, an initial 1,403 early trials rifles were converted to sniper configuration at the Enfield factory, but from September 1942 rifles selected after test firing were sent to the top London gunmakers Holland & Holland, where each was stripped and carefully rebuilt with a numbered scope and mount collimated to the rifle, each of which had its scope serial number stamped on the wrist of the butt stock. A cheek rest was added and every rifle supplied in a transit chest with scope tin, cleaning

The Enfield No.4 (T) rifle proved to be an unexpectedly good sniping weapon, particularly at longer ranges. Although the No.32 scope and its mount were a heavy combination, they were extremely hardy and were used on the post-war L42 rifle.

rod and oil, American M1907 leather shooting sling and manual. Some 26,442 were converted, the first seeing action in North Africa, where they performed poorly, mostly due to local weather conditions and lack of proper instruction. Yet the invasions of Italy in 1943 and France in 1944 gave the British snipers plenty of practice, although it was a hard game to learn, as many German snipers had gained valuable experience on the Eastern Front.

In use, the Enfield was arguably the best available rifle for long-range shooting, the bullet tending to stabilize more as the range increased. Canada too used the Enfield No.4 (T), but also fielded a number of Mk III Ross and Enfield P14 rifles with vintage Warner & Swasey scopes until such time as sufficient Enfields became available. Uniquely, Canada also manufactured its own No.32 scope, made by Research Enterprises Ltd, of Quebec. Australia had set up production facilities for its own sniping rifles, developing the venerable Mk III Enfield fitted with a Lithgow-manufactured heavy target barrel and Aldis Pattern 1918 scopes in claw mounts, a virtual copy of the German system widely used in World War I. It was a reasonably effective system, but of the 1,620 or so manufactured, few became available until near the end of the war.

Not that this situation bothered many Australian snipers working in South-East Asia, many of whom were professional kangaroo hunters and possessed patience, keen eyesight and the ability to snap-shoot using ordinary iron sights at distances of 300yds (274m). Charles Shore, a British sniping officer, wrote that:

> The Australian hunters are really remarkable shots ... probably the best of these were the kangaroo hunters ... they used the heavy barrel which is so popular. In Timor one of these kangaroo hunters was credited with 47 Japanese killed, but with characteristic modesty claimed only 25 certainties, remarking: 'In my game you can't count a 'roo unless you see him drop and know exactly where to go and skin him.'

Such feats were all the more remarkable because there was very little instruction offered to snipers – usually a basic course lasting a few days and in some cases not even that. One veteran sniper from Timor and New Guinea, who had been given a World War I P14 rifle with scope, said: 'My training was to read a little manual on using the scope then set up a target and work out how the damn thing worked.'

Despite shortages of rifles and limited training, the Allied troops fighting in the jungles managed to exact a high toll on the Japanese, particularly in counter-sniping work, where they found that teams using a sniper, light machine-gun and spotter were particularly effective. The LMG sprayed the treetops, often causing the hidden sniper to move, and the waiting sniper picked him off. It was slow work, but very effective, as the Americans were also to discover.

Military ball ammunition used from the beginning of the 20th century. From left: US .30-06in, British Mk.VII .303in, German 7.92mm Mauser (also known as 8x57mm Mauser); Soviet 7.62x54mm, French 8mm Lebel, Japanese 6.5mm. Many of these obsolete calibres can still be found in use around the world, and the Russian cartridge is still in frontline service.

AMERICAN SNIPER RIFLES

When the United States joined the war after the attack on Pearl Harbor on 7 December 1941, it had one of the largest and best-equipped armies in the world, but possessed no snipers or dedicated sniper rifles. Embarrassingly, the Army had submitted a report on 8 April 1941 to Washington stating that: 'No special training for snipers is contemplated … and no steps are being taken to procure special equipment. Special equipment is costly and requires special personnel to maintain and use it.' It was a decision that would come back to haunt the Army command.

The war had not been underway for long before the Army began quickly to rethink its sniping policy. A suitable rifle had to be found for the task, and the only logical solution was the M1903 Springfield, for it was available in large numbers and was reasonably accurate. Like all of its predecessors, though, it was conceived as a battle not a sniper rifle. Besides, no suitable telescopic sights existed and some method had to be found of converting the M1903s that was effective, practical and inexpensive.

Late in 1943, the Ordnance Department began testing scopes and decided on the 2.5x power Weaver 330-C, (soon renamed the M73B-1), which was available in quantity. It was mated to a commercial Redfield Junior bar mount that comprised a strong rail that ran above the breech, being solidly mounted on two blocks, one on the knox-form, the other on the rear receiver. Selected rifles were carefully gauged and barrels had to be near perfect, to within .001in internal tolerance, and converted rifles were named the M1903-A4. In practice, the Weaver was underpowered, the small rear-mounted range drum was fiddly to use and lateral adjustment had to done by the lock screw on the rear mount. On the positive side, it was simple, reasonably tough and, in the right hands, capable of 700–800yd (645–732m) shooting. One oddity of the 03-A4 design was the omission of iron sights from these rifles. In the event of

Sergeant Harry Furness, Normandy 1944

During the advance through France after D-Day, 6 June 1944, Sgt Furness often moved ahead of British patrols to gather intelligence on enemy positions and deployment. Usually this required the construction of a suitable hide and patient hours of observing. However, on occasion targets of opportunity appeared that were important enough to risk giving away his presence. On this particular occasion a German staff car disgorged a number of officers with field glasses and maps, and one man in the centre caught his attention. Although the range was around 600yds, Furness fired a snap shot, downing the officer. All hell broke loose as the Germans opened up with every weapon they had, including mortars and 88mm guns, twice blowing the sniper from his slit trench. When the firing died down, despite being dazed and deafened, Harry Furness slipped from his hide and wormed back through the smoking craters to return to his lines and report.

His Enfield No.4 (T) rifle was regarded by many as the best sniping rifle in use during the war, and as it was a particularly accurate rifle for longer ranges, a 600yd shot was not excessive. However, the sniper was dug in on a hillside so had to calculate not only the range and windage, but allow for the difference in bullet trajectory when firing from a high position. To do this with a split-second snap shot was extreme professionalism indeed.

damage to the scope, or the need for very close-range shooting, it rendered the rifle almost useless and while it did speed up production, the savings must have been minimal. One Army sniper recalled that: 'Most of us [snipers] carried an M1 [carbine] slung on our shoulder, it was a powerful fast-shooting little gun – perfect for close fighting which our Springfields sure weren't. Some carried the Thompson, but it was too heavy and I reckoned the M1 better by far.'

In reality, the Springfield was already on the verge of obsolescence when the war began, for the US Ordnance had been working since 1932 with a brilliant designer, John Browning, on a new infantry rifle, the Rifle, Calibre .30 M1 (Garand). It was a semi-automatic design using a gas recoil system and was introduced in 1936. By 1941 most infantry units were Garand equipped, but at the time no consideration had been given to creating a sniper variant. After endless testing by Headquarters, Army Ground Forces, a drilled and tapped bracket was fitted by the Springfield Armory to selected rifles and the M1E7 Griffin & Howe quick-release mount system was chosen, which used two quick-release levers to clamp the mount to the bar. Two commercial scopes were selected: either the 2.5x M73B-1 Weaver 330 or M73 Lyman Alaskan, and in mid-1944 some 8,300 Garands, designated the M1-C, had been ordered. Mounts had to be offset to the left, for loading the Garand was by clip only and this clip was automatically ejected when the last round was fired. Semi-automatic sniper rifles were complex and time-consuming to manufacture to sniper standards, as all parts had to be blueprint-perfect and hand-fitted. The M1-C was regarded as practical for sniping out to 700yds (640m) only, but using armour-piercing (AP) ammunition with its heavier bullet improved performance considerably. By the end of the war (August 1945) some 6,896 M1-Cs had been produced, but few reached the frontline. While it was too late for the war, it was to give sterling service in the not too distant future.

A US Marine poses with a new M1903-A4 sniping rifle. The modest size of the scope is clear – it was never powerful enough for long-range sniping. The decision not to fit iron sights is a puzzle, and was the reason many snipers carried carbines or submachine guns in combat.

The problem of finding suitable sniper rifles was much the same for the US Marine Corps, but the Marines had at least pursued their policy of competitive shooting at high levels. To this end they possessed a useful assortment of Springfield National Match rifles and a few Winchester Model 70 heavy-barrelled target rifles. Some of these were equipped with Winchester A5 or Lyman 5A scopes and others with the Unertl target scope.

The outbreak of war proved conclusively that fighting the Japanese without any sniper backup was costly, many Marines landing on the beaches of Guadalcanal finding themselves completely pinned down by accurate fire from invisible snipers. One said: 'our lieutenant called, "let's go men" and stood up on the bank in front of us. He was hit two or three times simultaneously by sniper fire and tumbled down. We stayed put, praying the tanks would move up.' The Japanese snipers used a 6.5mm or 7.7mm Arisaka that gave off almost no smoke or muzzle flash when fired. Fortunately, the small hardcore of experienced shooters within the ranks of the Marines enabled them to put together scratch sniper squads equipped with a somewhat motley collection of rifles, some with scopes but many without. They acquitted themselves well, but it was obvious that proper sniping rifles were needed.

The Marines examined their options objectively and came to the conclusion that the best way forward was also to adopt the existing Springfield. The decision was made to fit some Springfields with the commercial Unertl 8x scope, a very long-bodied target instrument of great power but considerable fragility. Rifles were specially selected then rebuilt by Marine armourers in Philadelphia using special 'C' type walnut stocks, with a pistol grip, polished internals such as magazine followers and feed ramps and blueprint-perfect barrels that were hand-bedded into the stocks. Trigger pull was carefully adjusted from the normal 6–7lb (2.7–3.2kg) to around 2–3lb (c.1.2kg).

Somewhere in the Pacific, a Marine cleans his Unertl-equipped Springfield rifle. Although overly long and delicate it proved its worth and the Unertl earned the respect of all who used it during the campaign, many seeing later service in Korea and Vietnam.

The Unertl was the most powerful scope then in military use (and would remain so until almost the 21st century), but its delicate sprung mounting system was the same as that used on Civil War sniping rifles and was easily damaged. Its length meant that the scope had to recoil backwards then slide forward (return to battery) when the gun was fired, and this action was compromised by use of a large spring around the scope body that jammed if dirt or sand entered the mounts. Despite these shortcomings, the combination of scope and rifle proved a good one; indeed the Marines and their use of Unertls have become iconic nowadays. There are many stories of these rifles being used at extreme distances, Private Dan Cass famously dispersing a Japanese machine-gun crew on Okinawa at a range in excess of 1,100yds (1,000m).

The problem with non-standard equipment such as the Unertl was performing field repairs, and Marine Ordnance ordered that their Springfields also be equipped with a smaller sight, so in late 1942 they adopted the M1903-A4 rifle, initially equipped with the same Weaver M73B-1 scope as fitted to the Army Garands. The pre-war Winchester Model 70s in use were also an excellent design and equally competent for hunting or target use. A number of them, equipped with Unertl scopes, were tested by the Marine Corps in 1941, but eventually rejected. They were perfectly capable of 1,000yd (914m) shooting, but the Corps believed that adoption of a non-standard rifle would further compound supply and repair problems. Nevertheless, some found their way to the Pacific in private hands, where their effective use in combat was not lost on the Corps. The Winchester would surface again, when the Marines broke radically with tradition by adopting the M70 as the first sniping rifle that was *not* a military-issue longarm.

As the war drew to a close, it became clear that, among the armies involved, there was no real consensus about what type of rifle was best for snipers. As in the previous war, the rifles in use were compromise weapons, converted infantry models of which none were ever designed with sniping in mind, and mostly fitted with commercial-pattern scopes that were insufficiently powerful. True, average sniping ranges had increased from 25 years previously, but long-range sniping was still the preserve of only a very few gifted snipers. Little had been done with regards to ammunition development either, for standard ball ammunition was generally used, although AP was proving to be a popular option when and if it could be sourced. But with the ending of the war came the belief that peace would be lasting and there was little will, politically or militarily, to continue the development of small-arms that would in all eventuality, never be required. How wrong this was will be the subject of the next chapter.

THE MODERN SNIPER

THE KOREAN WAR

If any thought at all was given to the development of sniper rifles in the years immediately after the war, it was not acted upon, at least by the Western powers. Yet in the wake of the Korean War, which erupted in June 1950, it would become clear that adapting existing service rifles was no longer an adequate policy. Much to the surprise of the American and Allied powers who were facing the Korean and Chinese troops over the 39th Parallel, the conflict quickly began to resemble the trench warfare of the Great War, and sniping became a very high-level activity.

The Chicom (Chinese communist) forces were well supplied with ex-Soviet M91/30 Mosin-Nagant sniping rifles, and they also possessed some very good snipers. None of the Allied forces had much in the way of either sniping rifles or snipers, and scratch sniping teams were hastily formed by the Commonwealth and US forces using a mixture of old and new. The Australians and New Zealanders had some venerable SMLE-based P1918 (T) rifles, Britain was able to field some No.4 (T) Enfields and the Americans gathered together a selection of Garand M1-Cs and M1-Ds, many still coated in the thick protective Cosmoline grease in which they had been stored, which took hours to remove. There was also a sprinkling of M1903-A4 Springfields with Weaver or Unertl scopes, and a new 4x power scope, the Stith-Killmorgen, began to appear, but in numbers too small to make any significant difference.

The old Unertls proved to be unexpectedly useful for a previously unconsidered problem, which was the extreme ranges often encountered in the high hills along which the front lines meandered. Here 800yd-plus (732m) sniping distances made it very difficult for many of the inexperienced

Allied snipers to register hits. Despite the belief that the Garand sniping rifles were inadequate for such ranges, they too could prove very effective in the right hands, Master Sergeant John Boitnott making nine kills with as many shots at ranges between 670 and 1,250yds (613 and 1,143m).

What was really required were weapons with the capability to shoot in excess of 1,000yds (914m), but few existed. Some Springfield/Unertl rifles were available, but they were too few and none were in the first flush of youth. Neither was there anything much in the way of sniper training, as one Marine recalled: 'As I was the only man in the company with any rifle team or shooting experience, the CO … requested a sniper rifle for me. "Hamilton, that makes you the company sniper."' While scratch training ranges were set up, the Army and Marines looked for rifles capable of shooting across the expansive Korean landscape, and providentially an Army Ordnance captain called William S. Brophy appeared. He had long been calling for the adoption of a dedicated target rifle for use in the sniping role, and he carried with him a .30-06-calibre Winchester Model 70 with 10x Unertl scope. Believing actions spoke louder than words, he toured the front lines, regularly shooting enemy soldiers at 1,000yds or more, but despite incontrovertible proof that shooting at this range was perfectly achievable, the US high command still clung to the belief that only a sniping rifle based on a military pattern rifle was acceptable.

Yet Brophy was not alone in his desire to extend the boundaries of sniping in a very real sense. After 1945, some tentative work had been done at Aberdeen Proving Ground, Maryland, with .50-calibre Browning barrels mounted in German PzB39 anti-tank rifles, but the experiments were not taken seriously at the time. The Army had also been playing with some captured Soviet 14.5mm PTRD and PTRS anti-tank rifles. Of very simple single-shot, bolt-action type, their heavy AP bullets had a velocity of 3,300ft/s

There is little apparent change since 1945 in the equipment being used by this Marine sniper in Korea. The only clue to the date of the war is his body armour, first introduced during the conflict and subsequently responsible for saving thousands of lives. His rifle is a World War II-vintage M1-C Garand with M82 scope.

(1,006m/s) and could penetrate 1in (2.54cm) of armour plate at 500yds (457m) as well as almost any steel sniper plate, concrete observation bunker or the most heavily layered wood and sandbag emplacements. In Korea, the biggest problem was finding sufficient 14.7mm ammunition, so a solution was found by fitting .50-calibre Browning barrels to the PTR actions. The Marines also borrowed some spare .55in Boys anti-tank rifles and ammunition from Canadian troops, then modified them by strengthening the actions with steel blocks to enable them to shoot double-charged .50-calibre ammunition. When mounted with a scope they worked very well and shooting at ranges of over 2,000yds (1,828m) was commonplace, 'to the acute discomfort of the Chicoms' as one observer dryly commented.

Writing as one who has fired a standard .55in Boys rifle and not ever wanted to repeat the experience, what a double-charged cartridge must be like to shoot can only be left to the imagination. There were, of course, insufficient PTR or Boys rifles available to permit this to be anything more than a useful experiment, but the Marines turned to what they had aplenty – Browning M2 heavy machine guns. It took little machining to manufacture a solid base mount that could be bolted to the top cover of the Browning and inevitably the Marines fitted the most powerful scope they had, the Unertl, in an experiment to see just what the .50-calibre cartridge was capable of. Like its bigger Russian brother, the Big Fifty or 'Ma Deuce', as it was fondly called, was a potent weapon. Firing an AP projectile weighing 706 grains (compared to 168 grains for the .30-06 rifle) at a velocity of 2,950ft/s (900m/s), it could shoot accurately in excess of 2,000yds (1,828m). Various unit armourers produced a number of examples, possibly as many as a couple of dozen, and while never officially acknowledged, these heavily modified AT rifles and machine-guns were to be the precursors of an entirely new generation of sniping rifles.

US soldiers in Korea pose with a modified Soviet PTRD anti-tank rifle. It has had a .50-calibre barrel fitted and what appears to be a Lyman Alaskan scope. Although only used experimentally, such rifles provided later manufacturers with extremely valuable data.

THE VIETNAM WAR

In a depressingly familiar move, at the end of the Korean conflict in 1953 sniper units were disbanded, soldiers returned to their units and rifles packed and stored. Post-war no Allied country involved in the fighting actually set up a proper sniper training course, as Western governments focused on the Cold War threat from the Soviet Union. It is easy to criticize those in command for their lack of foresight. Yet in the face of the inevitable cutbacks in military expenditure, and the fact that sniping had few high-level spokesmen within the military, it was inevitable that when in 1954 a small war in Vietnam suddenly became a much bigger one, no-one believed that there would be any requirement for snipers.

When America entered the conflict in 1961, it appeared that their involvement would be short and decisive, for the North Vietnamese Army (NVA) was not, after all, regarded as a major combat force. The US soldiers and Marines who flew into Saigon were mostly equipped with uniforms and weapons that would have been familiar to Pacific War veterans. Indeed, many of the officers and senior NCOs were veterans of that conflict, and plenty had misgivings about the lack of preparedness that the US military was showing in respect of sniping, particularly in the face of persistent Viet Cong (VC) sniping. Enemy snipers were not always competent, however. At Da Nang airbase, one enemy sniper, known as 'Five o'clock Charlie', would open fire at the same time every day, causing men to scatter, but seldom hitting anything. A plan to track down and kill him was abandoned on the basis that he was so inept it was worth keeping him in case he was replaced by someone who actually knew what he was doing.

US troops arriving in Vietnam were initially armed with the improved M1 Garand rifle, the M14, which was chambered for the new 7.62mm (.308in) NATO standard cartridge and usefully equipped with a detachable 20-round box magazine. Although uniquely the M14 had provision for a scope mount in the form of a threaded lug on the left side of the receiver, little work had been done in actually sourcing a scope and mount to fit. The situation was further muddied by the adoption of the new M16 rifle in 1965; the new rifle was designed for the NATO 5.56mm (.223in) cartridge, its tiny 55-grain bullet by no means a long-range calibre. This situation left the Army with a conundrum: either to retain a now obsolete

semi-automatic rifle as a sniping weapon, or source something entirely different to fill the gap. There was also the tricky problem of finding potential snipers, for there was still no training programme.

As usual, the Marines fared slightly better, as they had within the Corps many experienced competitive shooters, as well as ex-World War II snipers. There was still an acute shortage of suitable rifles, though, but when permission was granted in 1965 for the 3rd Marine Division to open a sniping school, the decision was made by Captain Jim Land to gather together every telescope-equipped rifle the Marines possessed. A motley collection of M1-C and M1-D Garands, M1903-A4 Springfields and the Marine rifle team's .30-06 Winchester Model 70s, with a miscellaneous assortment of scopes, was assembled and the snipers soon began to retaliate to the constant harassing enemy fire, racking up 60 confirmed kills in three months.

Yet there were simply not enough rifles to go around, so Brigadier General G. Van Orden placed an order with Winchester for the supply of up to 1,000 Model 70s with 24in (61cm) heavy 'varmint' barrels. These rifles were stripped by Marine armourers, re-bedded with glass-fibre and their barrels left free-floating. This process meant that from the breech onwards, no part of the barrel touched the stock of the rifle, eliminating pressure being placed on it by the enclosing woodwork, a common problem but one exacerbated by the heat and humidity found in Vietnam. Pressure adversely affected accuracy and was one of the reasons for the later widespread adoption of glass-fibre and plastic stocks. Poor specification barrels were replaced with new ones chambered for the 7.62mm cartridge, which of course required the supply of two different calibres of ammunition. For a while these Winchester rifles were to become the quasi-official sniper rifle for the Marines. Clearly, such a make-do policy was unacceptable, particularly as the military command in South-East Asia had begun to take an interest in snipers, not only for their ability to take the war to the enemy, but also as gatherers of information and intelligence.

A typical sniper team in the field, the rifleman with a Remington M700. (US Marine Corps)

Some decision had to be made with regard to the adoption of an acceptable, universal pattern of sniper rifle for multi-service issue. While the Winchesters were good, they were comparatively expensive and production of the Model 70 had ceased in 1965, when a new model was introduced. Neither were existing scopes well suited to jungle warfare. While the Army continued to use the old Garands and Springfields, their age was beginning to tell, and the Marines simply refused to accept them. They believed that what was wanted was a dedicated bolt-action rifle of 7.62mm calibre, with a scope tough enough to withstand the climate. It was not too difficult to find a suitable rifle. Remington had produced an excellent hunting rifle in the form of the Model 700, with a tough Mauser-based bolt-locking system, and after testing the Model 700 was adopted in April 1966 as the 'Rifle, 7.62mm Sniper, M40'. The 24in (61cm) barrel was free-floating, the wooden stocks were heat and vacuum treated to prevent the ingress of moisture, the actions were glass-bedded and all metal parts parkerized. Triggers were adjusted to a 4–4lb 8oz (1.8–2kg)

An M3 Sniperscope mounted on an M1 carbine during the Korean War. The scope and IR unit dwarf the rifle, and few infantrymen would want to have to carry the massive battery pack very far. But despite its bulk, the unit performed quite well, and some even saw service during the Vietnam War.

pull weight and magazine platforms and feed ramps were hand polished. The end result weighed a modest 9lb 8oz (4.2kg) with scope. At last, a new standard was being set for the military sniper rifle that was *not* based around an issue military rifle.

The biggest problem, as always, lay in the selection of a telescopic sight, as there were no existing military-specification scopes, therefore only commercial patterns could be sourced. After some consideration, Redfield's variable power 3–9x Accu-Range was selected. It was hoped that short-range sniping, commonplace in jungle areas, would be more easily accomplished with the scope set for 3x, while long-range shooting would remain uncompromised with the 9x resolution. In addition, the Redfield had a useful inbuilt range-finding scale. Generally, the Remingtons were capable of ½ moa accuracy (a half inch group at 100 yards), but many capable shooters could reduce this. Fears that the 7.62mm round would be underpowered were unfounded, as kills at 1,000yds (923m) soon became commonplace, Marine sniper Chuck Mawhinney dropping a VC insurgent at an incredible 1,500yds (1,372m), theoretically beyond the adjustment range of his scope.

Snipers were also belatedly being supplied with match-grade ammunition. This had theoretically been available in limited quantities since the early 1960s, but was, as one sniper said, 'like trying to get hold of horse feathers'. Made by Lake City Arsenal, the ammunition was initially fabricated in .30-06 calibre, but was soon available in 7.62mm NATO. It was referred to as M118 Ball Ammunition and was based on the 168-grain boat-tailed match bullet used in long-range shooting; it was a huge improvement over standard-issue ball ammunition. It was extensively used up to the early 1990s, when an improved cartridge would be introduced.

Meanwhile the Army Weapons Command had tried mounting scopes on the M16, but while competent enough out to 300yds (274m) or so, its tiny bullet was easily deflected by foliage or grass and could not provide longer-range accuracy. So they looked once again at the M14, and after a great deal of experimentation decided to use a factory-produced mounting bracket on the existing threaded lug and adopt the same Redfield scope as the Marines. However, the Army's scopes were modified by the installation of a cam system, developed by Lieutenant James Leatherwood, which automatically adjusted the elevation of the scope as magnification power was increased. These scopes, named the Auto Ranging Telescope (ART) series, were adopted in 1968 and the rifle and scope combination were named the XM21. Getting one to shoot accurately was not easy and involved blueprinting every component, welding up the gas cylinder to stop it unscrewing itself, fitting heavyweight match-grade barrels, polishing all internal parts, including the trigger bearing surfaces, and injecting stocks with resin to waterproof them. It was an expensive process, but the end result was a semi-automatic rifle capable of 1,000yds (914m) accuracy, with the added benefit of rapid fire in the event of close combat, a facility lacking with the bolt-action M40s. In the right hands it was very effective, as Army sniper Adelbert Waldron proved when he shot a VC soldier standing on the prow of a moving boat at a range of 975yds (891m).

STARLIGHT AND SILENCE

A continual problem facing the snipers was that of night fighting. Although the US forces were dominant during the day, at night they retreated to heavily guarded compounds, where they watched and waited, for the VC owned the night.

Although telescopic sights gather and enhance available light, making dawn and dusk shooting possible, they are of no more use than the human eye in complete darkness. In a small way, there had been some technical advances made regarding night vision during World War II. In February 1944, a prototype night-vision sight called the T3 'Sniperscope' was approved. It incorporated an infra-red converter tube and spotlight mounted on top of the rifle. This device further required a heavy battery as well, hardly conducive to stealthy movement, and although useful up to perhaps 150yds (137m) the sight made sniping impractical from anything other than a fixed position. Vietnam was nothing if not a fruitful place, for experimentation and development work continued into finding a night weapons system that was powerful as well as portable.

In the early 1960s, the AN/PVS-1 Starlight Scope was introduced, and rapidly went through a series of modifications to become the AN/PVS-2. This was to become the principal night-vision device for the rest of the war. It used an intensifier tube with photocathode lenses and phosphor screen, which magnified available light by 40,000 times. In fact, using one when there was any form of bright light was detrimental to both the sight and the shooter's eyes and it performed best in near total darkness or faint starlight. The Army found that by using a pink beam searchlight, it was possible to engage enemy patrols at 325–433yds (300–400m). One Marine sniper shot 14 VC sentries in succession using a night sight and silencer, a feat that would have been impossible just five years earlier. The only problem with the Starlight system was its inability to be mounted to the M40 rifle, so both Army and Marines used XM21s, which had a mounting bracket supplied with the scope. A number of M16 rifles were also adapted, as the scope proved very useful to snipers at the short ranges at which night targets were often engaged.

Early night-vision equipment was not compact. This photo shows a Vietnam-era Starlight scope mounted on a British L1A1 SLR rifle of the type used in the Falklands. Although effective, its weight and sheer bulk made it awkward to carry.

Of course, it was all very well being able to take the fight to the enemy at night, but betraying your presence with muzzle flashes and gunshots was inadvisable to say the least. A shot can be muffled using a suppressor, which disguises but does not eliminate the gunshot, whereas a silencer almost totally eliminates the gunshot, but requires low-velocity ammunition to do so. To work 100 per cent effectively, a bullet needs to be subsonic when used with a silencer and therein lay a problem, for subsonic ammunition was of use only at relatively close ranges of up to 150yds (137m). The silencing of rifles and pistols was by no means new science; Hiram Maxim had produced an effective silencer at the turn of the 20th century, but the tactical limitations imposed by silencing proved difficult to overcome. In the 1960s and 1970s, a great deal of work was carried out by the US Army Land Warfare Laboratory, in association with a company named Sionics Inc., to develop the Silent Sniper System.

Yet the stumbling block was always in finding a compromise between bullet performance and noise. Cartridges with reduced charges had to be packed with an inert material to take up the airspace in the case, with the result that the charge would either fail to ignite or, conversely, the cartridge might even explode. Most of the packing material used resulted in fouling that jammed semi-automatic weapons like the XM21, or required bolt-action rifles to be frequently cleaned. Accuracy was also compromised, as a silencer affected the harmonics of the barrel, altering its zero. Practical tests undertaken at the 23rd Infantry Division's sniping school during the war failed to achieve a measurable group on a 15x30in (38x76cm) target at 273yds (250m).

Although work on silencers/suppressors continued for the duration of the Vietnam War, a suitable system was never universally adopted, most sniper units retaining one or two dedicated suppressed rifles for night use. Besides, as one sniper pointedly commented, 'the best sniping was based on the principle of the further the better.' Furthermore, by the time the United States pulled out of South-East Asia in April 1975, both the Army and Marines had sniper training programmes firmly installed and the number of enemy accounted for by snipers was calculated to run into several thousand. Finally, it seemed the sniper was coming of age.

THE FALKLANDS LEGACY

Even before the Vietnam War ended, the United States was taking a long, hard look at the performance of its sniper rifles, as there was an open conflict between the need for firepower and the need for accuracy and range. Britain, meanwhile, had already decided to continue with a weapon design that was by then 80 years old. In August 1970, the British Army officially phased out the old .303in Enfield No.4 (T) rifles and introduced its replacement, a 7.62mm rifle with the nomenclature L42A1. In order to keep cost to a minimum, it was no more than an uprated No.4 rifle, with heavier barrel, shortened fore-end and improved No.32 Mk 3 scope with range drum graduated in metres not yards. It might have continued to be the frontline sniper rifle for many more decades, had not a small conflict begun in 1982 on a series of far-flung islands that most people had never heard of, the Falklands.

Although the Falklands War was not in itself a war of major military consequences, it was to sound the death knell for the British Army sniper's reliance on converted infantry rifles, and set in place a change that would revolutionize sniping within the British armed forces. During the extraordinarily soggy Falklands campaign, battalion snipers were hard pressed to deal with the numerous and often very good Argentine snipers, who were mostly armed with Remingtons. There were not enough British snipers to go around, and the L42A1s suffered from a lack of the cleaning materials that were required in the salt-laden atmosphere. The climate rusted actions, magazines and barrels, and despite the scopes being factory waterproofed, many still misted up badly. At least one British sniper, fed up with carrying his near-useless rifle, dumped it in a stream, picked up an Argentine FN FAL fitted with a short-range optical sight, and used it successfully for the duration of the campaign. So wanting was the sniping equipment that the Milan ground rocket system was found to be one of the most effective counter-sniping weapons, although each rocket would have paid for six new rifles!

After the war, it was clear that major improvements were needed, so following considerable testing the choice was down to the excellent Parker-Hale M85, a conventional bolt-action glass-fibre stocked weapon, and the rather less conventional AI sniper rifle designed by the late Malcolm Cooper, Olympic Gold rifleman. It was made by Accuracy International of Portsmouth. The end result, by the narrowest of margins, was the adoption of the highly adaptable Accuracy International rifle. Built around an aluminium rail chassis, the receiver was held by four screws and epoxy bonded to the chassis. The detachable free-floating stainless steel barrel screwed into the receiver, negating the need for time-consuming bedding. The polymer stock was two-piece, left and right, and simply screwed onto the chassis. The telescopic sights initially selected for the AI rifle were either a Schmidt & Bender PM 12x42, or Leupold 10XM1.

An early issue L96 sniping rifle, used by the Royal Marines during the First Gulf War. It is in its transit case with spare magazines, sling and cleaning kit. These weapons, inspired by the competitive rifles used for long-range target shooting, are constructed with a modular chassis, moulded stocks impervious to weather, and state-of-the-art optical sights. The Accuracy International family of rifles have set a new benchmark in military sniping.

Barrel manufacture had benefited hugely from advances in materials technology. In 1916 it was considered that a barrel was past its useful service life for sniping after 500 rounds, but by the 1980s the widespread use of stainless steel had increased this to 5,000-plus. Barrel twist rates had also altered. While the science is complex and often contradictory, generally there is an optimum twist for every calibre. Variables such as barrel length and bullet weight must be taken into account, but as a generality making a twist faster, i.e. increased from 1:10 to 1:9, will usually give the bullet a more stable flight and longer flight duration at supersonic speeds.

By the end of 1982 the rifle had been adopted for service, with the military nomenclature L96A1. It had a 656yd (600m) first-round hit capability (the ability for a sniper to reliably hit his target using his first shot, with a cold barrel and no sighting-in), and it was able to shoot accurately to ranges in excess of 1,190yds (1,100m). In 1988 an improved version, the Arctic Warfare (AW) rifle with a de-icing system, larger trigger-guard and stock thumbhole, was adopted by Sweden and Britain followed suit, naming it the L118A1. It had an uprated Schmidt & Bender 3–12x50 PMII scope which gave a larger image, better field of view and improved poor light capability. The rifles soon earned the respect of the snipers issued with them, in conflicts across the world. Bosnia, the Gulf Wars, Iraq and Afghanistan have all seen the L118 in hard combat and it has provided some remarkably accurate shooting. Corporal Chris Reynolds of the Black Watch waited three days in a hide for a chance to take a shot at a local Taliban warlord, who eventually appeared on a rooftop – 2,007yds (1,835m) away:

> I saw that he had a weapon, an AK47. We did all the calculations for range, wind speed ... I have to admit the first round landed next to him, but ... we were so far away that he didn't even realize he was being shot at. We changed our aim and when I took into account different factors like the trajectory of the bullet, my gun's scope was actually aiming at the top of a doorway. I fired and the bullet went off, coming down and hitting him in the chest.

In the wake of the Vietnam War, the United States had also reviewed its existing sniping rifles, and while they were pleased with the performance of their Remingtons the rifles required further upgrading. The Remington M40 had been modified in the early 1970s with the introduction of a glass-fibre stock, manufactured by Gale McMillan, and Winchester Model 70 trigger-guards and hinged-base floorplates (the latter enabled the magazine to be accessed easily). A lightened trigger assembly was added and 10x Unertl scope supplied, which incidentally was the first military scope to incorporate the mildot ranging system, a further explanation of which is given later. All the work was undertaken by Marine armourers at Quantico, Virginia, and the new rifle, now weighing a hefty 14lb 8oz (7kg), was officially called the Rifle, Sniper 7.62x51mm NATO M40-A1.

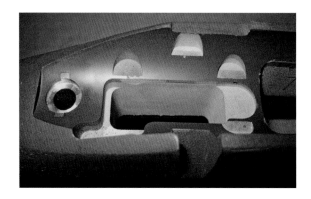

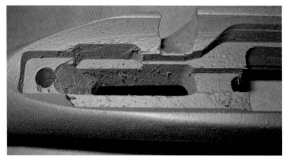

Two Remington stocks, showing the difference between a factory-standard model (bottom) and a hand-bedded example (top). The upper rifle has been filled with a layer of epoxy putty that raises the receiver and leaves the barrel free-floating. It is a time-consuming process but vital for creating an accurate rifle.

Not everyone was convinced of the superiority of the bolt-action sniping rifle, though. In 1963, the Soviet Union had adopted an AK variant, the Snayperskaya Vintovka Dragunova (the SVD or Dragunov) sniping rifle, which was a short-stroke gas-piston-operated, semi-automatic rifle chambering the old 7.62x54mm Mosin-Nagant cartridge. While it benefited from excellent optics, having a 4x PSO-1 sight with bullet-drop compensator and infra-red capability, it suffered from a lack of accuracy when used with ordinary military ball ammunition, producing on average 2.5in (65mm) groups at 656yds (600m). However, when used with high-quality 7N1 sniper ammunition loaded with a 158-grain spitzer boat-tail bullet, the accuracy improved to sub-1.5 moa groups, which represented 656–875yd (600–800m) hit capability on a human body and could extend to 1,300yds (1,200m) for support fire.

If nothing else, the Dragunov underlines the importance of using good-quality ammunition for sniping. The Russian Army retained the SVD and a number of models – the SVU and SVU-A, and VSS silenced models – sprang from its basic design. The reality, however, was that for long-range shooting the Dragunov design was limited so in 1998 the SV-98 was introduced. This was a bolt-action rifle designed along the lines of the AW, but capable of firing either 7.62x54mm or 7.62mm NATO ammunition. It is extremely accurate, its cold-forged barrel capable of almost ½ moa accuracy, but interestingly it did not supplant the SVD, but was used alongside it, specifically by counter-insurgency forces. Meanwhile, the Dragunov has been subject to a continual process of improvement, and the latest incarnation has black synthetic furniture and POSP 4x24V or 8x24V scopes that are nitrogen-filled to prevent misting and include illuminated crosshairs with a range-finding capability up to 1,000m.

OPTICAL IMPROVEMENTS

While it is easy to state that a rifle is capable of perhaps engaging a target at 650 or 1,300yds, this belies the very complex optical requirements behind such shots. In the two world wars, low-power commercial scopes were regarded as acceptable for military use, but in the latter part of the 20th century optical technology advanced out of all recognition. Advances in materials technology have enabled scope bodies to be transformed from thin steel or brass tubes to spun aluminium systems with complex shapes, and with lenses that are now computer-designed for any given requirement.

The Russian semi-auto 12.7mm OSV 96 rifle is equivalent to the .50-calibre rifles used by NATO forces. An unusual facet of its design is a barrel that is hinged at the front of the receiver and can be folded back to facilitate carrying, useful in a weapon that is 5ft 7in (1.7m) long. It was introduced in the early 1990s and has seen much subsequent use.

These lenses are machine-polished to a level of perfection once attainable by only a few highly skilled individuals. Ocular and objective lenses have also increased in diameter. Objective lenses have typically gone from 30mm to 50mm, providing the shooter with larger, sharper images that have an extremely wide field of view. Larger lenses also admit more light, enhancing the ability of the scope to be used in low-light conditions. Lens coatings, first introduced post-World War II, cut down glare and also improve light admission. Power has increased too, with some military scopes now having 25x magnification, to enable large-calibre rifles to be fired at great distances.

One of the smallest but most significant improvements has been the near universal adoption of the mildot crosshair, first introduced in 1915 for artillery use. A mil is a milliradian, which means it subtends 1yd of the circumference of a 1,000yd radius circle, or 1m of a circle of 1,000m radius, and the formulae for working out the exact distance is:

Range (metres or yards) = (Target size (metres or yards) x 1,000) / Size in mils, or
Range (in 1,000s of metres or yards) = (Target size (metres or yards)) / Size in mils.

A Russian SVD Dragunov rifle with PSO-3 scope. It has remained basically the same since its introduction and has proved its worth in conflicts around the world. In the exercise pictured, US Marines receive training on weapons found in Iraq and Afghanistan. (US Marine Corps)

The soldier in the crosshairs is blissfully unaware of his potential fate. Fortunately for him, this was a training exercise. In reality, he would never know what hit him. (US Marine Corps)

If you are not a mathematician, then a simpler explanation of the working of the mildot is that it works like a range-finder, because it equates (in metric) to half a metre at 500m. This can be taken as approximating an average man's shoulder width, so if a human figure two mils across would be at 250m, one mil across is at 500m and a figure at ¼ mil across would be at 2,000m. If (in imperial) a man is assumed to be 6ft (2yds) tall, and appears 5 mils high, then 2,000/5 = 400yds. When viewing an object of unknown size, the range can still be calculated if the object is compared to the mildot scale and a printed formulae is consulted. Although it requires some skill to master, the system is highly accurate and most military telescopic sights – Nightforce, Unertl, Schmidt & Bender and Leupold – still use it.

A new generation of thermal-imaging and image-intensifying devices is also available, such as the American AN/PVS models, British Kite and Norwegian Simrad, which mount independently on the rifle. The benefit of these systems is that the scope (and thus zero of the rifle) remains undisturbed. The AN/PVS series has continued to be developed, with the AN/PVS-22 (Universal Night Sight) now widely adopted for use with rifles. It is a far cry from the old T3 Sniperscope. Seven inches (17.8cm) long and 3in (7.6cm) in diameter, it weighs only 1.9lb (0.9kg) and has 40 hours of life from two AA batteries, but does cost $11,000. Thermal imaging has also become more sophisticated and compact, and leaves nowhere on the night-time battlefield for an enemy to hide. Widely used by international forces, the latest generation such as the PAS-13 is small enough to fit onto a sniper rifle and provides target identification up to 1,300yds, or 1,200m.

Even better news for the sniper is the common availability of laser range-finders. These are about the size of a packet of cigarettes but are accurate to +/- 1m at 1,000m; tripod-mounted ones can be used at ranges of up to 11 miles (20km). When the range-finder is equipped with a digital magnetic compass (DMC) and inclinometer, it is also capable of providing magnetic azimuth, inclination and height of targets. Increasingly, range-finders have a cable or wireless interface to enable them to transfer their data to other equipment, like fire-control computers. If the sniper is unable to engage the target due to size or distance, his observation data can be transferred instantly to a fire-control point for artillery or air strikes.

Bullet-drop compensators are not new – the Israeli Nimrod, PSO and ART scopes all used similar systems – but now electronic bullet-drop systems as well as laser range-finding are being incorporated into scopes as miniaturization gradually solves the problems of size and weight. A simple solution to the problem of mounting increasing numbers of accessories to rifles has been the introduction of the MIL-STD-M1913 Picatinny rail, a universal mounting platform now fitted to almost all NATO military small-arms.

The Remington lives on. Snipers zero their M40A2 rifles, using M118 Match ammunition. The M40s are fitted with Schmidt & Bender PMII scopes that have short Picatinny rails visible just above the elevation drum, as well as another forward of the objective lens. These enable the sniper to mount a wide range of laser, night-sight or thermal-imaging equipment.

Windspeed meters are also now commonly used. Aside from distance calculating, judging windspeed has always been one of the most difficult of skills, but electronic anemometers are now relatively cheap (about £70/$120) and are routinely carried by sniper teams. It should be stressed that such technology is still used only in conjunction with the sniper's own hard-learned skills, although increasingly it is being relied on to help speed up the training process.

THE GLOBAL WAR ON TERROR

Since the First Gulf War (August 1990–February 1991), coalition forces have been increasingly heavily engaged in fighting in the Middle East. After the liberation of Kuwait, the initial objective was the containment of Saddam Hussein and his reported nuclear/chem-bio threat, but following the terrorist atrocity in New York on 11 September 2001 and the US-led operations in Afghanistan and the invasion of Iraq in 2003, fighting has escalated in these two countries where there are now large numbers of Taliban and al-Qaeda forces.

At the beginning of this period, sniping proved to be a minority form of combat – during the whole of Operation *Desert Storm*, the Marine 1st Division snipers scored only 39 kills. In fact, this early conflict served mainly to highlight the technical difficulties of shooting at extreme ranges in desert and mountain conditions with conventional sniper rifles. While most of the coalition forces were using rifles chambering the 7.62mm NATO cartridge, however, the United States had introduced a major new player into the sniper's armoury.

In 1990, the Marine Corps purchased 125 M82A1 rifles from Barrett Manufacturing in Tennessee, chambered for the Browning .50-calibre cartridge. It was a shoulder-fired, short-recoil operated, semi-automatic anti-materiel weapon, with a 29in (74cm) barrel and an effective range of well in excess of 1,500yds (1,372m). Its mechanism relied on a barrel that recoiled for a short distance and an internal rotating-lock breech-block which had an accelerator arm that used part of the recoil energy from the

barrel to help push back the block on firing. This action cocked the firing pin and recycled the action, and as the block ran forwards it stripped a new cartridge from the ten-round magazine. The recoil generated by the considerable muzzle energy – 14,000ft-lb (18,970 joules) compared to the 2,648ft-lb (3,588 joules) of the 7.62mm round – was reduced by around 85 per cent through the weight of the rifle (a massive 30.9lb/14kg for the longer-barrelled version) as well as the use of large recoil springs and an extremely efficient muzzle-brake design. The recoil was still punishing, though, and some snipers who regularly shot such calibres suffered from back and shoulder problems and even detached retinas.

A Bausch & Lomb 10x40 telescopic sight from an L118 rifle, showing the added-on inclination angle drum (left). The reading needs a cosine calculation to be made, which then provides the shooter with adjustment figures for firing up or downhill. It is extremely useful in mountainous areas.

The US Army initially opted for a bolt-action variant, the XM107, but changed their minds in 2002, also adopting a semi-automatic variant, the Rifle, Calibre .50 M107. An improved version, the M82A1M, has since been purchased by the Marines and this has a full-length Picatinny rail over the receiver, as well as a rear monopod, slightly lightened mechanism and detachable muzzle brake. A special variant capable of shooting AP-incendiary Raufoss Mk 211 ammunition was also developed. Optics were initially Leupold Mk 4 3.5–10x40 Tactical, but the range of the Barrett required a sight of considerably greater power. Leupold now produce 8.5–25x50 scopes for long-range use, and these are being fitted to existing M82A1M rifles.

US Marine sniper team, Afghanistan 2009 (previous pages)

Increasingly, modern sniping is about observation and intelligence-gathering, and with their powerful optical sights and observation telescopes snipers are ideally placed for such work. While it can be mind-numbingly boring, it often results in the ambush of infiltrating Taliban or al-Qaeda fighters. In this illustration an observing sniper team of the 3rd US Marines has spotted a mortar crew attempting to set up their weapon for long-range shelling of a US base. At over 1,400m distance, the enemy has no idea they are under observation, let alone within striking distance of an aimed rifle shot. After requesting permission to engage, the sniper team took on the mortar crew, killing two immediately and then two more who attempted to run for the cover of a parked truck. Subsequent shots also disabled the vehicle, and a patrol established that it was laden with more explosives, which had the potential to become a vehicle-bomb or be used to manufacture an IED (improvised explosive device).

The .50-calibre M82A1 Barrett rifle is the most powerful sniping rifle in the coalition forces' armoury, and has the advantage of being semi-automatic, allowing fast follow-up shots that would be difficult with a bolt-action rifle. The limitations of optical sights and the difficulties of calculating windage and elevation at such distances officially restrict maximum combat ranges to 1,800m. However, it has been used successfully at ranges well in excess of this, and undoubtedly as optical technology improves this will rise significantly. The .50-calibre has not yet begun to near the limit of its performance.

Initially designed for destroying fixed installations, such as missile launchers, static aircraft and vehicles, the incredible performance of the .50-calibre rifle was soon appreciated by snipers, who made it the unequivocal king of the battlefield in terms of range and penetration. Concrete walls, brickwork, light armoured vehicles – none are proof against the massive power of the .50-calibre bullet. France also deployed a similar rifle, the bolt-action 12.7mm PGM Hecate, for long-range sniping, and during the Bosnian conflict it proved highly effective in counter-sniper work in built-up areas. Enemy snipers made great use of urban Bosnia's warren of tower blocks, but once spotted the building fabric proved no protection, as an unnamed French sniper later explained: 'When we found the hide of the sniper, we used two Hecates, firing as fast as possible. The debris generated by the flying concrete normally silenced [him], it was the same as throwing grenades into the room.' Although not conceived for use against human targets, these large-bore rifles give coalition snipers a definite advantage in engaging enemy snipers or observers at ranges beyond which conventional bullets could reach. Indeed, until November 2009 the greatest distance recorded for a sniper kill was with a US-made .50-calibre McMillan TAC-50 bolt-action rifle, chambering an M1022 long-range bullet. The kill distance was 2,657yds (2,430m), fired by Canadian Corporal Rob Furlong.

Current NATO sniping cartridges. Left, 7.62mm, centre .338 Lapua and right, .50-calibre BMG.

Yet it seemed clear that a compromise calibre between 7.62mm and .50 BMG was needed. Britain, which had tested the Barrett and had sanctioned the procurement of some AW rifles in .50 calibre for Special Forces use, turned to a little-known big-game hunting cartridge, the Finnish-made .338in Lapua. Loaded with a 300-grain hollow-point boat-tail bullet and producing a velocity of 2,710ft/s (826m/s), it had an effective range of 1,950yds (1,783m) and generated 4,892ft-lb (6,632 joules) of energy. It was quite capable of defeating body armour out to 1,100yds (1,000m), did not generate the recoil of the .50 BMG and, more importantly, could be used in most long-action rifles.

As a result of collaboration between Accuracy International and Lapua, Britain adopted the Arctic Warfare Super Magnum (AWSM) and in 2007 it was announced that the rifle, called the L115A3, would begin to replace the old 7.62mm series. It was equipped with a 5–25x56 Schmidt & Bender PMII sight, folding stock to ease carrying and a US-pattern Harris adjustable bipod. From the sniper's point of view, its comparatively light weight of 15.1lb (6.9kg) made it a far more practical proposition for fire and movement than a Barrett. Interestingly, it has since proven itself to be the match of the .50 BMG, and as of May 2010 the record for the longest-range kill is now held by British soldier Corporal Craig Harrison of the Household Cavalry, working in Musa Qala in Helmand province. Observing two Taliban machine-gunners who had opened fire on the unit's command vehicle, he fired his L1153A3 rifle beyond its accepted tactical range of

US-issue sniping ammunition, 7.62mm Match grade M118.

20 CARTRIDGES

7.62 MM MATCH
XM 118
LOT LC 12016

MATCH

BULLET 173 GRAINS
VELOCITY 2550 FPS

LAKE CITY ARMY AMMUNITION PLANT

Corporal Stefan Brouwers of the 2nd Dutch Marines zeroing an Accuracy L115A3 rifle in Afghanistan. The .338in L115 has proved hugely capable for long-range shooting, and some have even been supplied to the Russian Alpha counter-terrorist unit. (MoD)

1,640yds (1,513m) and killed both insurgents with two shots at a distance of 2,706yds (2,475m). In his own words: 'Conditions were perfect, no wind, mild weather, clear visibility. The first round hit a machine-gunner in the stomach ... the second insurgent grabbed the weapon and my second shot hit him in the side.' The complexities of such a shot are hard to comprehend, for Corporal Harrison had to calculate elevation and possible wind drift, and allow for the different air density at Musa Qala, which was 3,422ft (1,043m) above sea level. Furthermore, the flight time of the Lapua B408 bullet was three seconds. It clearly demonstrated that in terms of ballistic efficiency, the .338 gives little away to the bigger .50 calibre.

The American military have naturally exhibited great interest in the cartridge, and Remington have produced their own version of the AW, the Modular Sniping Rifle (MSR), which at the time of writing is undergoing testing in .338in Lapua and .300in Win-Mag calibres, and may soon be adopted by US forces. The Marines are now operating the third generation of Remington 700s, the M40-A3, with a heavy 24in (61cm) Schneider 1:12 twist stainless barrel (with a barrel life in excess of 10,000 rounds), Schmidt & Bender 3–12x50 scopes and Simrad KN200 night-vision sight. One shortcoming of these rifles is the fact that these have short-action receivers, unable to chamber the larger breed of magnum cartridges, so the Marines are also trialling the Iron Brigade Armory (IBA) XM-3 system. It is also based on the Remington action, but built to the highest possible specification with a suppressed Hart stainless barrel only 18½in (47cm) long (between 22in and 24in is usual for a sniping rifle), a McMillan adjustable stock, Nightforce NXS 3.5–15x50 scope and full maintenance kit. Despite the rifle's short barrel, fitted with its suppressor it is guaranteed to achieve an impressive sub-minute of angle three-shot group at 1,000yds (914m). The slight stumbling block is the price, which at a little under $19,000 is certainly expensive for any military bolt-action rifle.

The new Barrett M98B, chambered for the .338in cartridge. It weighs a reasonable 13.5lbs (6.7kg) compared to the .50 calibre's hefty 30.9lb (14kg). The .338's bullet performance is almost as good as the bigger cartridge, but without the recoil penalty.

Sergeant Jeremiah Johnson of the 1st Battalion, 23rd Infantry Regiment takes aim in Mosul, Iraq. His 7.62mm M24 SWS rifle is the last of the line that had its sniping origins with the M1-C Garand of 1944. As these rifles wear out, they are being replaced with the M110 SASS. (US Army/Sgt Jeremiah Johnson)

The US Army still fields the Remington M24 Sniper Weapons System (SWS), first adopted in 1988 and based on a Remington 700 long action that can chamber the new breed of magnum cartridges; the M24-A3 chambers the .338in Lapua round. This chambering capability offers the potential for uprating the rifle specification without huge cost implications, and the Army continued acquisition until early 2010 when a new semi-automatic weapon was adopted.

It may seem contradictory that despite the apparent preference within NATO for bolt-action sniping rifles, both Britain and America have simultaneously been looking at resurrecting the semi-automatic sniping rifle. The United States had continued with issuing the M14, now in use in the guise of the M21, as a Designated Marksman's Rifle (DMR), but the remaining 40,000 or so M14s in store had been used up and a replacement was needed. Britain too was struggling to provide extra firepower for use in FIBUA (fighting in built-up areas) situations, which in Iraq and Afghanistan were commonplace. The standard 5.56mm British L85A2 infantry rifle and US M16A3 have limited range and penetration and in the light of experience it was clear that a marksman's rifle was required that had a long-distance capability, but also the ability to generate considerable firepower in a combat situation. Thus it was decided that an accurized 7.62mm semi-automatic equipped with optical sights would bridge the gap nicely.

American Special Operations Command (SOC) units had for some time been using a Knight Armaments Mk 11 rifle based on the original Stoner AR10 design, which used the same basic gas-operation system as the well-established AR15 and M16s. The Mk 11 differed in being fitted with a 20in (51cm) heavy match free-floating barrel, two-stage trigger factory set for a pull of 4lb 8oz (2kg) and a breech-block that operates via a direct port in the barrel that catches expanding gas and uses the resulting pressure to drive back the block and bolt, cutting down on parts and increasing functional reliability. The barrel can also accept a suppressor, something the M21 semi-automatics could not do. With a Leupold 3.5–10x30 sight mounted on the Picatinny rail, bipod and loaded ten-round magazine (it will also take a 20-round magazine), it weighs a fairly substantial 16lb (7.3kg), which is almost an average weight for a modern service sniper

Testing the opposition. An Iraqi-made Tabuk sniping rifle. These are locally manufactured Yugoslavian RPK rifles, normally equipped with the OM-M76 4x telescopic sight, chambered for the Russian 7.62x54mm cartridge. It is not a high-precision weapon, but good enough for sniping out to approximately 656yds (600m).

rifle, though many snipers believe it is too heavy. Adopted for general issue as the M110 SASS (Semi-Automatic Sniping System), it has proven capable of ½ moa shooting and at its normal service range of 656yds (600m) will consistently group within 3in (7.6cm). With special ammunition, it is capable of engagement out to 1,100yds (1,000m) and the Army first issued it for service in Afghanistan in April 2007. It has since become the issue sniper weapon for the US Army, supplanting the M24 rifles; while the Marines use the Mk 11 model, although still retaining their much-loved Remington rifles.

Britain has followed suit, having decided on a variant of the M110 made by the Lewis Machine and Tool Company of Milan, Illinois, to be supplied by Law Enforcement International of London and designated the L129A1. It has a contact ability out to 980yds (900m) and like the M110 SASS has the ability to accept a wide range of accessories. It will replace the ageing Accuracy International 7.62mm bolt-action rifles. One ex-sniper the author spoke to agreed that such a weapon was much needed. 'A 5.56 is just not up to engagements over 300m, while the L96 is too slow and anyway they [the Taliban] target anyone carrying a long rifle. This will provide far better firepower at longer distances. It's well overdue.' In a first for the British Army, the initial 440 guns will be issued to Designated Marksmen, who will not be trained to full sniper level but have the skills to enable them to engage out to 900m.

CONCLUSION

In a little under a century, the sniper has emerged from the shadows to become the most highly trained and expensively equipped frontline specialist, second only to Special Forces. Never before has the training and equipping of snipers been such a high military priority, particularly at a time when military budgets are under considerable strain. What is also interesting is the change in attitude towards snipers on the battlefield. From the first deployment of riflemen in the 18th century, sharpshooters and snipers had long been regarded by the world's military forces as no more than a temporary and rather unpalatable expedient. It is only now that the world's armies have come to realize that the sniper is a vital component in forming a cohesive military strategy. Snipers have become the eyes and ears of the battlefield, as much intelligence-gatherers as combat soldiers. Their ability to distinguish between friend and foe, particularly in modern urban war where the line between insurgents and civilians has become completely blurred, means that they are often the only ones able to take the fight to an otherwise invisible enemy. It is for good reason that both Iraq and Afghanistan have been dubbed 'snipers' wars', and as a result there has been far greater media interest paid to them than in the past. Indeed, the sniper has become almost a cult figure, the subject of countless internet articles and several Hollywood films.

The shooting abilities of the modern sniper would seem incredible to a sniper from World War II, and the durability, accuracy and power of modern rifles are beyond anything in use even a decade ago. At what rate this expansion of technology will continue is unquantifiable, but I suspect that rather than slow down, it will continue to speed up. It is true that the cost of training snipers is very high, and attempts are being made to reduce the lengthy training period, currently six weeks in the UK, to four. In part this may be achievable by using increasingly sophisticated technology (i.e. laser range-finders), but this may well start the retrograde process of

The author with his venerable, but still extremely accurate 1943 Enfield No.4 (T) rifle. (Author's collection)

replacing skill with technology. There is also a very real danger that current training will be based on the wars now being fought, while overlooking the fact that future wars may well be very different in form. Nevertheless, the resurgence of the sniper has been one of the great military success stories of the 21st century. It is perhaps a small comfort to know that in an age where sophisticated technology is the new God on the battlefield, one infantryman with an accurate rifle and a cartridge costing 25 pence is still capable of dominating a battlefield.

APPENDIX

Specifications of primary sniping rifles mentioned in text

The effective range quoted is taken as that considered to be the maximum possible range for a guaranteed hit on a human body by a competent sniper. Some snipers could improve considerably on this, depending on conditions. The weight given is an average for an unloaded rifle with standard pattern scope and mount.

Berdan Sharps Model 1859
Type: Single-shot capping breech-loader
Calibre: .52in
Barrel length: 29in (73.7cm)
Weight: 7lb 8oz (3.5kg)
Muzzle velocity: Appx. 1,400ft/s (436m/s)
Effective range: 500yds (457m)

Mauser Gew 98
Type: Bolt-action
Calibre: 7.92mm (8x57mm) rimless
Barrel length: 29.1in (74cm)
Weight: 10lb (4.5kg)
Muzzle velocity: 2,850ft/s (870m/s)
Magazine type/capacity: Internal, 5 rounds
Effective range: 500yds (457m)

Mk III Lee-Enfield
Type: Bolt-action
Calibre: .303in rimmed
Barrel length: 25.2in (64cm)
Weight: 10lb 2oz (4.6kg)
Muzzle velocity: 2,400ft/s (731m/s)
Magazine type/capacity: Box, 10 rounds
Effective range: 600yds (553m)

Enfield P14 (T)
Type: Bolt-action
Calibre: .303in rimmed
Barrel length: 26in (66cm)
Weight: 11lb (5kg)
Muzzle velocity: 2,400ft/s (731m/s)
Magazine type/capacity: Internal, 5 rounds
Effective range: 700yds (640m)

Enfield No.4 (T)
Type: Bolt-action
Calibre: .303in rimmed
Barrel length: 25.1in (64cm)
Weight: 11lb 8oz (5.4kg)
Muzzle velocity: 2,400ft/s (731m/s)
Magazine type/capacity: Box, 10 rounds
Effective range: 700yds (640m)

Mosin-Nagant M1891/30
Type: Bolt-action
Calibre: 7.62x54mm rimmed Soviet
Barrel length: 28.7in (73cm)
Weight: 9lb 6oz (4.3kg)
Muzzle velocity: 2,680ft/s (795m/s)
Magazine type/capacity: Internal, 5 rounds
Effective range: 600yds (553m)

Mauser K98k
Type: Bolt-action
Calibre: 7.92mm (8x57mm) rimless
Barrel length: 23.6in (60cm)
Weight: 9lb 10oz (4.1kg)
Muzzle velocity: 2,450ft/s (745m/s)
Magazine type/capacity: Internal, 5 rounds
Effective range: 600yds (553m)

Springfield M1903-A4
Type: Bolt-action
Calibre: .30-06in rimless
Barrel length: 24in (61cm)
Weight: 8lb 12oz (3.8kg)
Muzzle velocity: 2,800ft/s (853m/s)
Magazine type/capacity: Internal, 5 rounds
Effective range: 600yds (553m)

Garand M1-C/M1-D

Type: Semi-automatic, gas-operated
Calibre: .30-06in rimless
Barrel length: 24in (61cm)
Weight: 10lb 8oz (4.9kg)
Muzzle velocity: 2,800ft/s (853m/s)
Magazine type/capacity: Internal, 8 rounds
Effective range: 700yds (640m)

Model 70 Winchester

Type: Bolt-action
Calibre: .30-06in rimless
Barrel length: 24in (61cm); 20 and 26in (51 and 66cm) available
Weight: 7lb 12oz (3.5kg)
Muzzle velocity: 2,800ft/s (853m/s)
Magazine type/capacity: Internal, 5 rounds
Effective range: 1,000yds (914m)

Springfield Armory XM21 (M21)

Type: Semi-automatic, gas-operated
Calibre: 7.62x51mm NATO rimless
Barrel length: 22in (56cm)
Weight: 11lb 10oz (5.2kg)
Muzzle velocity: 2,800ft/s (853m/s)
Magazine type/capacity: Box, 5, 10 or 20 rounds
Effective range: 750yds (685m)

Remington M40A1

Type: Bolt-action
Calibre: 7.62x51mm NATO rimless
Barrel length: 24in (61cm)
Weight: 14lb 8oz (6.7kg)
Muzzle velocity: 2,800ft/s (853m/s)
Magazine type/capacity: Internal, 5 rounds
Effective range: 800yds (732m)

SVD Dragunov

Type: Semi-automatic, gas-operated
Calibre: 7.62x54mm Soviet rimmed
Barrel length: 24.5in (62cm)
Weight: 9lb 8oz (4.3kg)
Muzzle velocity: 2,723ft/s (830m/s)
Magazine type/capacity: Box, 10 rounds
Effective range: 800yds (732m)

M110 SASS

Type: Semi-automatic, gas-operated
Calibre: 7.62x51mm NATO rimless
Barrel length: 20in (51cm)
Weight: 15lb 4oz (6.9kg)
Muzzle velocity: 2,571ft/s (783m/s)
Magazine type/capacity: Box, 10 or 20 rounds
Effective range: 800yds (732m)

Accuracy International AW L96A1

Type: Bolt-action
Calibre: 7.62x51mm NATO rimless
Barrel length: 25.6in (65cm)
Weight: 13lb 4oz (6.1kg)
Muzzle velocity: 2,788ft/s (850m/s)
Magazine type/capacity: Box, 9 or 10 rounds
Effective range: 1,200yds (1,100m)

Accuracy International L115A1

Type: Bolt-action
Calibre: .338in Lapua Magnum rimless
Barrel length: 27in (68.6cm)
Weight: 15lb 2oz (6.9kg)
Muzzle velocity: 2,800ft/s (853m/s)
Magazine type/capacity: Box, 5 rounds
Effective range: 1,500yds (1,372m)

Barrett M82A1

Type: Semi-automatic, recoil-assisted
Calibre: .50in BMG (12.7x99mm) NATO rimless
Barrel length: 29in (74cm)
Weight: 28lb 5oz (12.9kg)
Muzzle velocity: 2,788ft/s (850m/s)
Magazine type/capacity: Box, 10 rounds
Effective range: 1,500yds (1372m)

SELECT BIBLIOGRAPHY

Chandler, N. A. and Chandler, R. F., *Death From Afar*, vols 1–4, Iron Brigade Armory, Jacksonville, FL (1993–98)

Hogg, I. V., *The World's Sniping Rifles*, Greenhill, London (2006)

Law, R. D., *Sniper Variations of the German K98k rifle*, Collector Grade, Cobourg, ON (1996)

Pegler, M., *Out of Nowhere: A History of Military Sniping*, Osprey, Oxford (2005)

Pegler, M., *Sniping in The Great War*, Pen and Sword, Bradford (2009)

Senich, P., *The German Sniper 1914–1945*, Paladin, Boulder, CO (1982)

Senich, P., *The Complete Book of US Sniping*, Paladin, Boulder, CO (1998)

Skennerton, I., *The British Sniper*, Skennerton, Margate, UK (1984)

Plasterer, Major J. L., *The History of Sniping and Sharpshooting*, Paladin, Boulder, CO (2008)

INDEX